ESTRENO Collection of Contemporary Spanish Plays

General Editor: Martha T. Halsey

THE BELLS

OF

ORLEANS

ANTONIO GALA

THE BELLS OF ORLEANS

(Los buenos días perdidos)

Translated by Edward E. Borsoi

ESTRENO
University Park, Pennsylvania
1993

ESTRENO Contemporary Spanish Plays 4
General Editor: Martha T. Halsey
            Department of Spanish, Italian and Portuguese
            College of the Liberal Arts
            The Pennsylvania State University
            University Park PA 16802 USA

Library of Congress Cataloging in Publication Data
Gala, Antonio, 1936-
    The Bells of Orleans
    Translation of: Los buenos días perdidos
    Contents: The Bells of Orleans
    1. Gala, Antonio, 1936-   Translation, English
I. Borsoi, Edward E. II. Title
Library of Congress Catalog Card No.: 93-71911
ISBN: 0-9631212-3-5

© 1993 Copyright by ESTRENO

Original play © Antonio Gala 1972

English Translation © Edward E. Borsoi 1993

First Edition
All rights reserved
No part of this publication may be reproduced or transmitted in any form or by any means, electronic or mechanical, including photocopy, recording, or any information storage or retrieval system now known or to be invented, without permission in writing from the publisher, except by a reviewer who wishes to quote brief passages in connection with a review written for inclusion in a magazine, newspaper, or broadcast.

This play has been translated with financial assistance from

The Spanish Dirección General del Libro y Bibliotecas
of the Ministerio de Cultura

Cover: Jeffrey Eads

A PLAY THAT RINGS THE BELL

Playwriting is a special discipline which involves some very rigid demands: a play must be entertaining. The very mention of the word *entertainment* is enough to raise the hackles of some of my academic colleagues. "Entertainment? You mean as in *SHOW BUSINESS*?" These are the same people whose only criterion of literary worth is the amount of intellectual density per square inch.

Not that I am less demanding. In evaluating a dramatic work I often use the word *substantive,* by which I mean that something interesting is said about the human condition. Therefore, I am happy to report from my dual viewpoint as a working dramaturge and as a practicing director that *The Bells of Orleans* is both substantive and dramaturgically stage worthy. Not only does Gala successfully use the events in the play to dramatize the cultural and spiritual emptiness that underlies the material progress of contemporary Spain, but he does it with full use of the dramatic potential of the characters and the given circumstances.

Consuelito is a uniquely interesting character, both simple-minded and witty. Her dreams of being free from the chapel that encloses her are compelling enough to motivate her eventual fate. All the characters operate on several levels. Hortensia is basically amoral while maintaining a facade of strict morality. Lorenzo sees himself as a dreamer, but his flight at the end reveals his true lack of fiber.

But Gala is at his best dramaturgically when he has Consuelito lead us with charm and wit through the successive revelations of the profundity of her desires to the eventual outcome. She climbs the bell tower and "flies off to Orleans."

So, a toast to Gala--an artist sensitive to the plight of his fellow human beings, and one who, luckily, has the playwriting skill to dramatize it for performance on the stage.

      Robert O. Juergens
      Dramaturge, Annie Russell Theatre
      Rollins College

GALA: *LOS BUENOS DÍAS PERDIDOS* ("THE BELLS OF ORLEANS")

It is not often that a play comes along with such a skillful and generous blend of character and allegory as Antonio Gala's *The Bells of Orleans*. This rich, lusty fable tells the story of a quartet of characters caught in a changing and uncaring world.

Hortensia, who used to run a "private house for young ladies," and her son, Cleofás, have opened a barber shop in the ancient "right wing of the church," formerly the chapel of Santo Tomé, surviving by selling off the treasures of the church and remodeling the chapel into a home for their enterprise. They empty the tombs of treasure and fill the church with modern conveniences: a crock pot, a refrigerator, a washer-dryer.

Hortensia is a tough old bird with very little compassion. Her son, Cleofás, who in seminary dreamed of "converting pagans," now settles for the role of chapel caretaker and passes the time exchanging philosophy with those in need of a haircut. His wife, a simple but lovely girl named Consuelito is the true spirit of the play. She is a former circus contortionist who was abandoned by her father, a circus performer who used to saw her mother into four parts. Now she is stuck in the church playing serving girl to her husband and mother-in-law, but she still dreams of escape: "Why does everybody have to be doing what they don't like? Life is short and we have to spend it getting screwed!"

As the play opens, Consuelito sits frosting a box of cardboard stars. Out of nowhere a stranger arrives, the handsome and charismatic bellman, Lorenzo. He comes to Santo Tomé looking for a home. But he has a dream: to play the bells in Orleans. Consuelito, who dreams of escaping her circumstances, warns Lorenzo not to say anything to anyone about his dream. This is a house where dreams are stolen.

In *The Bells of Orleans* the rape of tradition takes place, not with sudden violence, but with slow and painful betrayals. Consuelito and Hortensia are seduced by Lorenzo's dreams. Lorenzo makes promises to each, but in between the dream and the daily drudgery lies the truth. When Lorenzo finally leaves, he takes with him more than a stolen bell. "Life doesn't play tricks on us. Dreams play tricks on us" says Cleofás. In the end, it is the dream of Orleans that tricks the now pregnant Consuelito as she climbs the bell tower for the last time.

This is a script which longs for the stage. Its colorful characters and sense of place are part of an allegorical kaleidoscope both fantastic and familiar. The language is filled with humor and insight. The action, from Consuelito demonstrating her contortionist act to the final ringing of the bells, takes us on a journey that can only occur in the theater.

>						Jeff Storer
>						Artistic Director
>						Manbites Dog Theater
>						Durham, North Carolina

(Jeff Storer directed a presentation of *The Bells of Orleans* in 1990)

Antonio Gala

ABOUT THE PLAYWRIGHT

Antonio Gala was born in Cordoba in 1936. By 1957 he had earned three university degrees: in Law, Philosophy and Letters, and Political Science. His deep interest in religion led him to enter a monastery for a time after finishing his studies. He has directed art galleries and collaborated on musicals and operas. These diversified acts are manifested in his writing. He has been one of contemporary Spain's major playwrights and the most commercially successful of those who write works of serious intent. He has received numerous awards, among which are the National Literary Prize and the Spectator and Critic's Prize. In 1990 he won the prestigious Planeta prize for his first novel, *El manuscrito carmesí* (*The Crimson manuscript*)

Gala began his literary career in the 1950s as a poet and short story writer. He later became a national celebrity for his various magazine and newspaper columns and his televised series on Spain. Gala entered the theatrical scene triumphantly in 1963 with his prize winning play *Los verdes campos del Edén* (1963; Eng. trans. Patricia O'Connor, *The Green Fields of Eden*), a socio-political satire of Franco's Spain. His other major plays include *Anillos para una dama* (1973; *Rings for a Lady*), a new perspective on El Cid, Spain's national hero, and his wife, Jimena; *¿Por qué corres, Ulises?* (1975; *What Makes You Run, Ulysses?*), a modernized and witty demythification of the Ulysses and Penelope story; and *Petra Regalada* (1980), a political allegory that sustains his feelings for feminist vindication. Gala's most recent theatrical work were two librettos he wrote: for *Carmen Carmen* (1988), a musical which satirizes Spanish male types, and for *Cristóbal Colón* (1989), an opera written to commemorate the quincentennial of the discovery of America.

Gala is admired as a stylist for his ready wit and the poetic quality of his prose. Among the themes of his plays are the search for paradise and the demythification of heroes or supposed saviors. Both of these are evident in *Los buenos días perdidos* (*The Bells of Orleans*). The play was an immediate hit, earned a series of major awards, and ran for more than 500 performances. It was revived in 1991 for another successful run.

Phyllis Zatlin (adapted)

CAUTION: Professionals and amateurs are hereby warned that *The Bells of Orleans,* being fully protected under the Copyright Laws of the United States of America, the British Empire, including the Dominion of Canada, and all other countries covered by the Pan-American Copyright Convention and the Universal Copyright Conventions, and of all countries with which the United States has reciprocal copyright relations, is subject to royalty. All rights, including professional, amateur, motion picture, recitation, public reading, radio and television broadcasting, and the rights of translation into foreign languages, are strictly reserved. Particular emphasis is laid on the question of readings, permission for which must be secured in writing.

Inquiries regarding permissions should be addressed to the author through the
    Sociedad General de Autores de España
    Fernando VI, 4
    28004 Madrid
    Spain
or through the translator.

Los buenos días perdidos was first staged at the Lara Theatre in Madrid on October 10, 1972, under the direction of José Luis Alonso.

STAGE SET

The ancient chapel of Santo Tomé, situated in the right wing of the transypt of a sixteenth century church. The construction has been clumsily adapted for housing.

On the left, a doorway to two bedrooms. Downstage on that side there is the beginning of a staircase that leads to the bell tower. On the right, a door which leads to the church. A sofa-bed, a small trunk, etc. Set in the wall, a tombstone.

Upstage, the entrance from the street, with an undefined pointed arch. An improvised barber shop, with a rotating chair, some barber shelves, a mirror. The door to a bathroom, jutting out toward the front. And, in the left corner, a space designated as a kitchen, covered with a curtain.

Here and there, modern furniture, of the mass produced type, in bad taste. A refrigerator. A table. A lot of plastic, a lot of formica and a lot of mediocrity.

The contrast between the original construction and the later additions must be drastic and almost shrill. Just seeing it should set one's teeth on edge.

CHARACTERS

Consuelito
Hortensia
Cleofás
Lorenzo
Don Remigio *(voice only)*
Don Jenaro *(no speaking part)*

ACT ONE

SCENE I

CONSUELITO, *sitting in a low wicker chair, which is her own little chair, is applying silver frosting to some cardboard stars. She has by her side a box full of them and is surrounded by everything she needs for such a delicate operation. She occasionally wipes her silver-stained hands on her hair. She is singing.*

CONSUELITO:

>Mariblanca! Mariblanca!
>Got knocked on her butt!
>And the bull stuck his horn
>In her you-know-what.
>
>Mariblanca! Mariblanca!
>Once more in the dirt.
>And the bull shoved his horn
>(He shoved his big horn)
>Up the poor girl's skirt.

(LORENZO enters through the door to the street with a suitcase in his hand, looks at CONSUELITO a minute; he leaves the suitcase on the floor; on tiptoe he crosses toward the doorway which leads to the bell tower and disappears. Soon afterward the ringing of the Angelus bell is heard. Half-distracted, CONSUELITO murmurs:
"The Angel of the Lord declared unto Mary and she conceived through the word and grace of the Holy Ghost..." *Suddenly she realizes how unusual it was for the bells to have rung. She gets out of her chair and looks up, startled. In her chair she leaves the star she was frosting. The Angelus bell stops ringing. LORENZO comes down. They look at each other. LORENZO goes toward CONSUELITO.)*
LORENZO: Good morning.

(CONSUELITO answers with a vague and frightened sound and falls back into her chair. LORENZO, to calm her down, starts to put his hand on CONSUELITO'S half-silvered head. She gathers in her shoulders, like someone expecting a blow. LORENZO starts to take his hand away.)

CONSUELITO: No... don't take your hand away yet. *(Slight pause.)* All right, now you can. Thank you.
LORENZO: What are you doing?
CONSUELITO: *(Still nervous.)* Making stars... Or don't they look like stars?
LORENZO: *(With his hand to his right ear.)* What?
CONSUELITO: For Christmas.
LORENZO: But it's already January.
CONSUELITO: They're for next Christmas.
LORENZO: What? I'm a little hard of hearing in this ear.
CONSUELITO: *(Ingratiating herself.)* Well, you're doing just fine. On Mondays, Wednesdays and Fridays my father couldn't hear a thing either. *(She looks for the star she was working on.)*
LORENZO: Your father, who's he?
CONSUELITO: A good-for-nothing.
LORENZO: Are these for the parish?
CONSUELITO: No, sir. For the general public. The biggest ones cost twelve pesetas. The others are three.
LORENZO: How many have you got?
CONSUELITO: Two-hundred and twenty-five. *(Pulling out from underneath her the star she had sat on.)* Well, two hundred and twenty-four.
LORENZO: Would you sell me one of the small ones?
CONSUELITO: Retail?
LORENZO: If I bought two, would they multiply between now and December?
CONSUELITO: No, no sir; wouldn't that be great? Stars are sterile, like mules. Here, take this one; it's really nicely finished... *(She starts getting more relaxed in the midst of her nervousness.)* Before, I used to make wigs. But they would turn out like this, a little lopsided. And Doña Hortensia used to say I ruined a lot of hair by getting it in the soup... but the hair in the soup came from the customers... *(She points to the barber's chair.)* Not from my wigs... This frosting business is a lot neater.
LORENZO: You work pretty fast.
CONSUELITO: Well, I'm used to it. I just can't wait until Christmas comes again...! At Christmas the house is nice and clean, without a single star... It's a pleasure to see.
LORENZO: You have beautiful hair.

CONSUELITO: Oh sure, beautiful! You're really a smooth talker... Since they don't buy me any turpentine, I have to wipe my hands on my hair. I must look like a tramp.
LORENZO: What?
CONSUELITO: A tramp, a streetwalker.
LORENZO: Who?
CONSUELITO: Me.
LORENZO: You're a tramp?
CONSUELITO: You must really be hard of hearing.
LORENZO: Don't I know it...
CONSUELITO: Talking to you is like talking to a wall. But now that we're on the subject, who are you?
LORENZO: I'm the one who rang the Angelus bell.
CONSUELITO: But how did you get to the bell tower? That's the only staircase...
LORENZO: I came down from heaven.
CONSUELITO: Well, you made a big mistake. Because things around here... *(She makes a Bronx cheer.)*
LORENZO: *(With his hand to his ear.)* What?
CONSUELITO: *(She repeats the Bronx cheer.)* Agh, damned deafness. We'll have to see how well you ring the bells. You obviously don't do it by ear, because... Bells make good company, don't they? When I was a little girl I wanted to be a stork. Ever since I've been here I've always said: this parish, without a bell ringer won't go anyplace... Things need...
LORENZO: *(Interrupting her.)* You're not from here?
CONSUELITO: Me? No, sir. Not on your life. *(Going back to her thoughts.)* Things need publicity. Think about it: a circus has its big parade. And who doesn't like circuses? All the more reason for a church to have something like that since it's a lot less fun... You wouldn't be from the circus, would you? *(Wrapped up in her thoughts.)* I really love a good carnival. A nice funeral isn't bad either but where there's a circus, with elephants, half-naked ladies and a juggler...
LORENZO: Where are you from?
CONSUELITO: *(Insulted.)* From nowhere. In my family, we've all worked the fairs. Except for an aunt who became a nun... What about you?
LORENZO: My father was a lighthouse keeper.
CONSUELITO: Wow, that's pretty silly... Well, a lighthouse and a bell tower are about the same thing. Just think: you're the kind that stays in one spot and we go wandering around; from one bunch of clowns to

another... What a life! *(Wrapped in thought.)* At first we would go as a troupe. My mother was called Zoraida. They used to cut her in four parts, inside a box, with a saw. My father was the one who would saw her: he was a great hypnotist. But one day he tried to saw her for real and my mother jumped out of the box screaming. And the next day... Boom... off and running with the lion tamer.
LORENZO: Your mother?
CONSUELITO: No! My father! With a rocket up the ass, you might say.
LORENZO: Who? The lion tamer?
CONSUELITO: My father! And he probably still has it, unless they removed it.
LORENZO: But, who put the rocket up his ass?
CONSUELITO: It's just a figure of speech. What did you have in mind? My father was quite a man. Such a man that we got here fifteen years ago and we're still here. My mother and I, that is; we got ditched like a pair of old socks. Then my mother went and set herself up as a fortune teller. She used to say: "To tell the future, one town is as good as another. All you have to do is know how to put on a turban." Because, you see, she used to put on a purple turban with a feather here. She looked pretty...
LORENZO: You're pretty, too.
CONSUELITO: Oh, come on! The trouble with you is that you're quite an artist yourself.
LORENZO: I think you're very pretty.
CONSUELITO: Well, I thought your hearing was bad. But compared to your eyesight, it's terrific.
LORENZO: How about you? Did your mother ever tell you your fortune?
CONSUELITO: Oh, she never was on target with the family. It was all right with the customers since we wouldn't be seeing them again. But with the family... I could tell you that after my father left us she kept setting the table with three plates... Every day for seven years she would say "Today is the day. He'll be back before the day is over." And until we finished dessert she wouldn't let me have my father's soup, which by that time was pretty cold...
LORENZO: Didn't you have an act of your own?
CONSUELITO: Of course. I was a contortionist. What happened was, when I was nine I hit my head on a curbstone and banged my brains... Hey, why am I telling you all this? It's because you're new... In this house nobody pays any attention to me. I never speak. Here, it's as if I were dead. It's as if I went to sleep one night and the next morning I

wanted to wake up but I couldn't. "But, Consuelito, girl, you're just dead" I say to myself all the time. Nothing ever happens around here. Nothing. That's why I'm nervous... It's not that I'm stupid all the time; I'm just nervous. I heard the bells... A little thing like that, almost nothing--ding, dong, ding, dong--was what I was waiting for... And besides that, I'm really happy you're so deaf because that way I can shout, which is what I like. I wanted to be a bell ringer. I wanted to be everything. But Doña Hortensia broke my dreams: she says that bells are only good for calling cows... *(Pause.)* Could you show me how to ring the bells? *(Holding out her hands, which he takes.)* Would I be any good at it?

LORENZO: Yes... Consuelito.

CONSUELITO: Well, how did you know my name? You're pretty clever, aren't you? Anyway, it won't be because I lack agility. I still have plenty left. *(She has lowered two ropes from which, in an earlier time, two lamps were apparently suspended.)* Shall I give you a demonstration?

LORENZO: Of what?

CONSUELITO: Of contortionism. You didn't think I was going to hang you, did you? *(Eagerly.)* You want me to do it for you?

LORENZO: Well, if it's up to me... *(He nods approval. CONSUELITO begins to perform a silly, not very difficult, routine. And she continues in accordance with the dialog.)* Very nice!

CONSUELITO: You like it, don't you?

LORENZO: It's great. You ought to do it for a living.

CONSUELITO: In the beginning, Cleofás used to say I was terrific in bed. That I seemed like another person. Not him; he doesn't seem like another person. What about the drum? Do you know how to play the drum?

LORENZO: *(Apologizing.)* No...

CONSUELITO: Because this routine comes off a lot better with drum music. I really go for somersaults and a lot of jumping through the hoop, which is my specialty. This business with the stars! Lord, what I always say is why does everybody have to be doing what they don't like? Life is so short and we have to spend it getting screwed..., really screwed!... Did you know I've been to Barcelona? You don't do much traveling, do you? Naturally, because of your job. You can't be expected to take your bells from one place to another.

LORENZO: When it comes to traveling, I've always had a dream.

CONSUELITO: *(Amazed.)* Oh, a dream! Me, too! Can I tell you about it? Forgive me if I do all the talking, but if I don't tell you about my dream, who would I be able to tell it to? Then you can tell me yours... Doña Hortensia and Cleofás aren't in my dream at all. *(She begins to act out her entire narration.)* A girl comes out in front of a bunch of soldiers dressed in blue. She has loose, long hair--very long, and red. How sad! She's standing in one spot, moving her arms like a windmill, as if she were swimming. But the girl is the only one who's alive. And suddenly, she has to start running, with her skirt around her waist. Run! Run! *(Calling out in back of her.)* I have some dimples here, just like a little kid. And I start dragging my long hair through the water, like the tail of a kite, and I start crying like this... because the bows in my braids get soaked.

LORENZO: But I thought you were wearing long, loose hair.

CONSUELITO: Well, you know how crazy a little girl's hair is. *(Transition.)* In the part in her hair she's wearing a star *(Showing disdain for the cardboard stars.)*, but it turns out to be a starfish. And it's ready to eat her up. Only nothing happens. Finally, she goes to the circus. She turns around and goes in. There's a chimpanzee in pajamas who's dialing telephone numbers. It's the tightrope walker's son. Strange things happen in the circus. Cleofás says they're always doing something wild. Maybe you know something about that since you dream, too.

LORENZO: My dream is different. It's something else; a wish I have, something I need to do before I die.

CONSUELITO: Ah, yes. Live! *(Disillusioned.)* What good does it do? Did you know that sea turtles spend a lot of time speaking with the stars at night? *(LORENZO will keep on shaking his head, indicating no to her, getting more and more overwhelmed. She speaks to him like one child to another, with the same kind of seriousness.)* Did you know that if you have a cup of warm soup it's easy to die suddenly? Did you know that if you do whatever you want, they wind up hanging you? Well, then, I don't understand you. What the hell do you want?

LORENZO: Me? I want to ring the bells in Orleans.

CONSUELITO: *(Fascinated.)* Hey, now that is something new. Where is Orleans?

LORENZO: Far away. Far from here. In another country.

CONSUELITO: Well, I haven't been there. I didn't even know they had bells in other countries. I thought they were worse than us. You never can tell. *(Encouraging him to speak.)* But go on, go on. Do you mind if I do my routines while you talk? Once I get going...

LORENZO: *(Imitating CONSUELITO in a deliberate game.)* Do you know that if you dream about bells that are swayed by the wind you'll have an

accident? *(CONSUELITO will keep on shaking her head no, almost hypnotized.)* And, that if they ring in your dreams it's a sign that somebody's saying bad things about you? Do you know that if owls fly around a bell tower, the parish priest is in danger of dying or that some sacrilegious theft is going to take place?
CONSUELITO: *(Secretively.)* A sacrilegious theft? Oh no...
LORENZO: *(As she did previously.)* Well, then, what the hell do you want?
CONSUELITO: Me? I want you to keep on talking to me, but don't mention that kind of theft...
LORENZO: You see, Consuelito, when my father used to whack me, I would say: "It doesn't matter. I'll ring the bells at Orleans and I'll leave everybody with their mouths wide open." When he wanted me to become a lighthouse keeper, I would say: "What for? I was born to go to Orleans to ring the bells..." When I was in the seminary...
CONSUELITO: You were in the seminary, too?
LORENZO: Yes, with your husband; but I flunked out. I enrolled so I wouldn't have to stay in the lighthouse...
CONSUELITO: Well, you jumped out of the frying pan into the fire.
LORENZO: Until I realized that wasn't the way to get to Orleans.
CONSUELITO: Of course not! Orleans is something special.
LORENZO: So I left. Since then I've been ringing bells here and there... Especially in small towns. For religious festivals and local celebrations, for pilgrimages...
CONSUELITO: Just like a rookie bullfighter. You poor thing!
LORENZO: And I've forgotten about Orleans. You start going down the road, more and more roads, until you don't even know where you're going...
CONSUELITO: Ah, but don't fool yourself; the important thing is the road. By the way, what's your name? Well, what do I care? Getting there is always the same. The towns and the people are the same... *(Conceding.)* I don't know anything about Orleans... But the road, oh, God. My father used to say "Look, Consuelito, look at the thick blossoms on those olive trees. This is going to be a good year for oil." Of course, they were oak trees, but what's the difference? We were meant to go around and have somebody tell us things about the countryside. Even if they're lies. Because not even the country is important. What's important is us, walking, and the other person putting his hand here. *(On her shoulder.)* And saying to us: "Hey, Consuelito, look..."

LORENZO: *(Putting his hand on her shoulder.)* Hey Consuelito, look: today I remembered Orleans again. It's getting to be too late for us to do all the things we've lived for... *(Pause.)*
CONSUELITO: Hey, you're starting to get sad on me. But you're in your prime. You remind me a lot of Jorgito, who was the strongman and had muscles like this... Man, I don't like you acting like a jerk... *(LORENZO lets himself be consoled.)* Ah, life! Life is a drag. And you came in here like a ray of sunshine through the window. Just like an angel of the Lord.
LORENZO: You're the one who's an angel.
CONSUELITO: Come on, you're going to make me pee in my pants. If I were an angel, what the hell would I be doing in this house? I would fly in the air like this... like this... and I would go... to Orleans. *(She stops. She takes some stars and twirls around until she runs into DOÑA HORTENSIA, who comes in from the street.)*
HORTENSIA: Cut it out! You two-bit carny! You side-show freak! Cut-it-out! *(She pinches Consuelito, something which she will do often.)*
CONSUELITO: Ow! Ow! I just couldn't stop...
HORTENSIA: I'll stop you. Do you think you're in the public square showing off your belly button like when we picked you up? *(As she goes to drop off the grocery bag which she has in her hands, she sees LORENZO. She changes her tone, a frequent occurrence with her.)* Let's show a little respect for this sacred place, Consuelito, dear. Were you the one who rang the Angelus bell?
CONSUELITO: No. It was this gentleman.
HORTENSIA: *(To LORENZO.)* My son will be right back. He went to see the Bishop. You can wait for him. Did you want a haircut or a shave? I can start heating the water...
LORENZO: You must be Doña Hortensia. I'm Lorenzo, Cleofás's friend. I told him I was coming.
HORTENSIA: Oh yes. How foolish of me, Lorenzo... *(Evidently impressed.)* I didn't know you were so... tall. Please forgive her bungling. You've probably figured out that the poor thing... *(A gesture that CONSUELITO is crazy.)* A cross we have to bear. We can handle it, but there are some days... When the weather changes she gets... Why don't you frost some more stars, honey? You really rang the bells beautifully. I was at the market and I thought I was in seventh heaven. Now if you have that same smooth touch with everything that you have with the bells... *(LORENZO smiles sheepishly. Perhaps he didn't hear. She takes a bottle of wine out of the grocery bag.)* Around here nobody

drinks but the doctor ordered me to have a little something with my meals. I've lost all my appetite. And the thing is, I have an appetite when I sit down at the table, but as soon as I start eating, I lose it. *(Modestly. She takes off her coat. Lorenzo helps her and hangs it on the coat rack.)* Would you like a little drink while you're waiting? *(CONSUELITO makes some funny gestures as she hums, because she knows that LORENZO is not understanding anything.)* I'll join you to keep you company... Stop singing!
CONSUELITO: I was only humming.
HORTENSIA: Well, don't hum. Can't you see that the gentleman and I are having a conversation?
CONSUELITO: Yes, Yes. But the gentleman...
HORTENSIA: She's a bit crude. It's a good thing you're like one of the family, because we all have to be very careful. You've already seen what a neighborhood this is: all atheists. And those that aren't might as well be, since they don't contribute any money to the parish... And you wouldn't even want to hear about the rumor-mongers.
CONSUELITO: *(Smugly.)* Talk louder to him. He's a little deaf... from the bells.
HORTENSIA: You could have told me before I got carried away, you shithead. *(In a penetrating shout.)* So then, what brings you here?
LORENZO: *(With a grin that leads us to believe he is not so deaf.)* I applied for a job as a policeman and they gave it to me. They told me that this was a very peaceful community... and since Cleofás was here, well...
HORTENSIA: Oh, it is, my boy, it is. I should say so. And we're delighted that you're here. We could really use a good friend who's on the police force.
LORENZO: At your service. *(Going along with her.)* All for one and one for all... Right?
HORTENSIA: *(Hypocritically.)* That's right: we're all brothers and sisters. What about the bells? Are you going to forget about them?
LORENZO: That's the way life is. Between the low salary, the people who don't care for music and the electronic carillons, the profession is just about finished. It's not what it used to be. There's no one who feels a calling for it. Now the people that ring the bells are plumbers, coalmen, bricklayers, firemen... It's all the same: a lot of neon lights in the churches, a lot of central heating, a lot of microphones, a lot of gaudiness... and when it comes to the bells, to hell with them. In all of Spain there are only two of us left who are good bellmen. And the other one was a drunk who...

HORTENSIA: *(In a lower voice she will use when she wishes to hide some comment from LORENZO.)* Well, poor old bells: one man drunk and the other without eardrums...
LORENZO: It's an art that just doesn't pay well...
HORTENSIA: I know: the world we live in is so materialistic. This is not my generation... Well, for my age it is. What I mean is that I'm different, more spiritual. All my life, the men in my house have belonged to the army or to the church. It's been a tradition, as it should be. The same thing with my in-laws. You see, my husband...
CONSUELITO: Was he a priest?
HORTENSIA: *(In a low voice.)* You slimebag. *(Aloud.)* He was a telegraph operator. But very religious. And my cousin, Sebi, who was superbright, went into the army. The only thing I can say is he got to be a top sergeant. Now he's in Argentina. As a matter of fact, I just found out today, through this letter. *(She shows it to him and puts it in front of him.)* See, it's from Argentina. He went there because he had the misfortune of being a top sergeant in the Civil War, but with the Commies. Anybody can make a mistake. You don't think things out well and... But from what he tells me he made a fortune... I'm ultraconservative but I know how to forgive. From my appearance you probably can tell that I haven't always lived like this... Can't you?
LORENZO: *(Wittily.)* You can tell from a mile away, Señora. That pride, those hands...
HORTENSIA: You really do understand... But, my friend, they're not even a shadow of what they once were. My house was a grand house, of the upper middle class, as they always say, even though in most cases it's not true. *(A pained smile.)* Our table was always so elegant, the salmon we served was happy to be there... What hors d'oeuvres, what fun! We spared no expense. It's not that I miss it. Every parrot has its parasite, that's what a Cuban friend of mine would say. He looked a lot like you: sort of lanky, maybe a little darker...
LORENZO: What did he say?
HORTENSIA: Every parrot has its parasite.
LORENZO: And what is that supposed to mean?
HORTENSIA: I don't know but he used to say it a lot. I've always been very devoted to my memories. *(The telephone rings.)* Excuse me. *(She picks up the receiver.)* Hello... *(Very dryly.)* This afternoon. You can come this afternoon before the rosary. *(She hangs up.)* I don't know where it's all going to end. One of those penniless bums, who calls up by telephone, no less, to see if he can come and get his hair cut. I tell

you, this neighborhood... Could you really believe that most of them use toothbrushes? Or that their kids graduated from high school? I think they're all communists... You can understand why we really can use a policeman. Less fighting and more donations, that's what we need around here... My Cleofás makes a living with the barber shop and his Latin classes. The poor thing can't keep up. I would have preferred a bar--a nice little bar. I could have tended it myself. That wouldn't make me swallow my pride. And Don Remigio, the parish priest, was all for it. But Cleofás didn't dare try it. He's such a fussbudget. He said that the barber shop was more decent. And since we're here in the right wing of the church... Before this it was the chapel of Santo Tomé, but with a little bit of praying we were able to get certain concessions from Don Remigio. Life is such a constant struggle...! *(Referring to the tomb.)* You see that? The founder. *(Reading from the gravestone.)* "Here lies the body of Doña Leonor Carrillo de Velasco, Countess of Albolafia...
LORENZO: ... who, in order to assure greater promptness, stands erect to await her resurrection."
CONSUELITO: *(In her own thoughts.)* The old girl was crazy.
HORTENSIA: You get back to your galaxy, dear... *(Referring to the tombstone, on which an image of the Countess is sculptured.)* All very elaborate. People with money have always been the same: they live well, but when it comes to dying... they die even better. Look, look. Lord, what extravagance. What squandering on rings and necklaces. *(Attentive to LORENZO'S reaction.)*
LORENZO: *(As alert as she is.)* Yes, indeed, it's a real waste.
HORTENSIA: So much baggage for such a small resting place... Speaking of resting places, where are you staying?
LORENZO: I don't know yet. I just got here. My suitcase is over there.
HORTENSIA: Well, stay with us. It'll be cheaper for you and you'll be taken care of better than in a boarding house. They're all so gloomy and falling apart. *(CONSUELITO lifts her eyes toward LORENZO.)*
LORENZO: I wouldn't think of it. You're here as a family... And Cleofás probably wouldn't like it. We haven't seen each other for a long time; he must have changed.
HORTENSIA: Nonsense. It'll be fine. Cleofás will do what I say, as always. That way you can ring the bells from time to time. Besides, I'll put in a word to Don Remigio to make you the official bellman. You'll have a small salary. Something modest, but...

LORENZO: Thank you, Señora. Thank you. A million thanks. *(He slyly goes over to kiss her hand.) HORTENSIA sighs and points out the sofa to him. A slight pause.)*
HORTENSIA: This is your bed. It'll be like sleeping on a cloud... It's a lot more practical than the ones I used to have in my house... Do you remember?
LORENZO: No. I was never there.
HORTENSIA: *(Who has already seen through him, but who likes him.)* Seven feather beds with canopies, which made them look like floats at the Holy Week procession. Sit down, sit down. *(She sits down.)*
LORENZO: I don't want to be a nuisance in such a nice house...
HORTENSIA: You're not a nuisance at all. I love being able to speak with someone educated, even if you're deaf. Aren't you going to sit down? *(LORENZO sits. The bed creaks threateningly.)* Don't worry. *(She holds him back because he goes to get up.)* Cleofás will fix it; he's very handy. I'm sure your bed was trying to give you a warm welcome. And, my boy, I can see why. *(She sighs and drinks.)* But have a drink... I remember when my first husband... well, my husband, proposed to me, his stomach started growling. He was older, and pretty impetuous: a Basque, no less. And I told him: "Don't get all worked up about it, Paco. Remember, the way to a girl's heart is through your stomach." *(A fit of laughter. She observes LORENZO's seriousness.)* Did you hear me? *(He nods.)* The old saying about the way to a man's heart is through his stomach... Don't you get it? Oh, Jesus!... Well, have a drink, at least.
CONSUELITO: You'll wind up drowning him... Of course, by now your glands are soaked like rum cakes.
HORTENSIA: Quiet, bigmouth... *(To LORENZO.)* What a burden! *(She sighs.)* While we're waiting for Cleofás I'll fix something to eat... It seems as if my appetite woke up and I don't want it to fall asleep on me. Doctor's orders. I'd just let myself waste away. You can't imagine how delicate I am... *(To CONSUELITO.)* You, did you put the beans on? Look at her: with her legs spread apart; she looks like a country bumpkin... Did you put them on or not? *(She pinches CONSUELITO.)*
CONSUELITO: *(Somewhat afraid.)* No, Señora, I forgot.
HORTENSIA: You ought to be boiled in oil.
CONSUELITO: Because I like to eat snacks... I go for fritters and potato chips. Every night at nine o'clock my father used to say that beef stew was to blame for the Civil War.
HORTENSIA: I'd like to know who your father was.

CONSUELITO: Well, he was a very cultured man. And very bright and into everything. Just so you might know, he began a career as a teacher twice. And he was from Pamplona itself.
HORTENSIA: Oh, shut your trap, you sap.
CONSUELITO: Hey, that rhymes.
HORTENSIA: *(To LORENZO.)* We were just talking about the household chores. She forgot to do something. *(Referring to CONSUELITO.)* It's a good thing there are so many conveniences today... Because that's one thing we have for sure... Listen... *(In a lower voice.)* That is, if you can, because nothing I say... Our crock pot, our refrigerator, our washer-dryer, our everything. Today, you live much better than before. Well, I don't. The riffraff does, you know. In order to know how to walk on carpets you have to pee on them first and Lord knows, I've done my peeing. But, do you remember those pine tables? How awful!
CONSUELITO: *(Almost behind her.)* You used to scrub them with lye and the knots in the wood would start coming out. Like a bunch of old relatives.
HORTENSIA: Now we have formica, which is elegant and comes in different colors...
CONSUELITO: *(Sadly.)* Even if you wanted you can't get any stains on it.
HORTENSIA: Everything in plastic. Today you wash any old pot and it's like new. Ah, just like the men in the old days... We've got the church so full of flowers it's like a garden, a flower garden. All in plastic.
CONSUELITO: It makes you hesitate to go in... *(She goes toward the bathroom. HORTENSIA moves closer to LORENZO.)*
HORTENSIA: Since life has now left me only flowers and candles...
CONSUELITO: *(From the bathroom.)* Doña Hortensia, how many pairs of panties did you put in the dirty clothes this week? I can only find one...
HORTENSIA: *(Having had her bubble burst, and with a gesture of deep resignation.)* You'll find out when I get a hold of you! *(Referring to the church.)* I'm going to pay a visit. I'll be right back, Lorenzo, and welcome.
LORENZO: It was a pleasure meeting you, Señora.
HORTENSIA: *(To CONSUELITO.)* Don't let me see you talking to him, you tricky bitch. *(She goes into the church. CONSUELITO and LORENZO look at each other and smile.)*
CONSUELITO: *(Into his ear.)* Is it true that you're going to stay here?
LORENZO: *(Holding the star from the beginning of the act.)* Yes, Consuelito, it seems you gave me the lucky star. *(LORENZO puts his hand on CONSUELITO'S head, and she drops the star that she has taken*

to frost. The poor thing sighs strangely. DOÑA HORTENSIA comes in with one of the Stations of the Cross under her arm. When LORENZO sees her he moves away from CONSUELITO.)
HORTENSIA: Here you are, dear. Take this to Matilde.
CONSUELITO: Is this to pay for the groceries?
HORTENSIA: Don't ask any questions. Just take it to her.
CONSUELITO: In the last year or so we've eaten up half the Stations of the Cross.
HORTENSIA: This is one of the three "Falls of Christ." *(Said to LORENZO, who is scrutinizing it.)*
CONSUELITO: It's a good thing there's more than one. Because before long, making the Stations of the Cross in this church is going to be like taking the express train: no stations to stop at. *(She is combing her hair in front of the barbershop mirror.)*
HORTENSIA: All right, let's get going. You're not going to get that face looking any better by combing your hair... Get out of here... Good Lord!
CONSUELITO: *(As she leaves, to LORENZO.)* Don't say anything to anybody in this house about the bells in Orleans... Because if they find out... *(She makes a snatching gesture to indicate theft.)* Remember, it's not just castanets you play...

(CONSUELITO leaves. LORENZO and HORTENSIA look at each other face to face. They smile, knowing each other's intentions. CONSUELITO sticks her head in the door and sees them.)

DARKNESS

Los buenos días perdidos, Lara Theatre, Madrid, 1972. Dir. José Luis Alonso. Setting designed by Francisco Nieva. Photo by Manuel Martínez Muñoz. Amparo Baró, Manuel Galiana, Mary Carrillo, and Juan Luis Galiardo.

SCENE II

CLEOFAS, dressed as a barber with a white smock, finishes cutting DON JENARO'S hair. The latter only nods affirmatively or negatively with his head, gravely and solemnly. HORTENSIA and LORENZO are sitting around the table. CONSUELITO is nearby, in her chair.

CLEOFAS: Italy is a country that's lost faith in itself because it's lost faith in the truth. Right, Don Jenaro?
DON JENARO: *(Nod of approval.)*
HORTENSIA: My God, listen to him speak. Listen to him speak... What a great preacher he would have made, or what a great politician... When you come to think of it, they're both the same.
CLEOFAS: When men no longer try to be free they put themselves in the hands of those who offer them a mirage of security... A man who's not free suffers from mirages, just like in the desert... Isn't that so, Don Jenaro?
DON JENARO: *(Affirmation.)*
CLEOFAS: There are nations that have lost their dignity as nations. They've given up. They live off of charity. They ask others to guide them, like blind beggars, no matter where.
DON JENARO: *(Negation.)*
CLEOFAS: Excuse me, Don Jenaro, excuse me. *(Showing him his haircut with a hand mirror.)* Is it all right like that? *(On the other side.)* Eh?
DON JENARO: *(Affirmation.)*
CLEOFAS: It turned out really nice around the neck, Don Jenaro. *(DON JENARO begins to get up.)* Thank God, Spain has regained its sense of empire and like that mythological goat called Amaltea, she can suckle--if you'll pardon the expression--she can suckle worlds once again. *(In the meantime he has been brushing him off.)*
DON JENARO: *(Affirmation, nodding his head twice.)*
CLEOFAS: That'll be twenty pesetas, Don Jenaro. *(He accompanies him to the door.)* Good day, Don Jenaro. At your service, whenever you wish, Don Jenaro. *(The customer leaves.)* Consuelito, clean up a bit. *(CLEOFAS takes off his smock. CONSUELITO starts to obey.)*
LORENZO: I'll help you.
HORTENSIA: *(Stopping him.)* Don't be silly. Let her do it. That's what she's here for.
LORENZO: *(To CLEOFAS.)* This Don Jenaro, is he mute?
HORTENSIA: No, he's not mute. I don't know what the hell he is...

CLEOFAS: Mama... The thing is he just doesn't talk. He only nods his head yes or no.
LORENZO: *(To CLEOFAS.)* That's a little weird, isn't it?
CLEOFAS: He says he's Catholic but anti-clerical.
HORTENSIA: There you go. As if God, by being God, wasn't Catholic and super-clerical. What that guy wants, like so many others, is to protect himself from the hordes with religion and, at the same time, not give a cent for worship and the clergy. I know all about it...
CLEOFAS: Mama.
HORTENSIA: Sure, Mama. Instead of cutting his hair you should cut his throat once in a while.
CONSUELITO: *(While she sweeps up the hair.)* Great. Do you know how hard it is to clean up blood?...
HORTENSIA: Keep sweeping and keep quiet... He's a priest-killer in disguise like others I know. If it were open season on priests again, you'd see. That's what I always say to this one here. *(She's speaking of CLEOFAS. She almost always speaks to LORENZO.)* Why do you talk to him? Let him go get a haircut in a masonic lodge or a synagogue or whatever...
CLEOFAS: Mama, you can't cut somebody's hair without talking to him. That's bad taste. *(To LORENZO.)* And since nowadays you can't mention football or bullfights without hurting somebody's feelings...
CONSUELITO: Especially the bullfights: when you mention horns, every husband...
HORTENSIA: What do you know! *(CONSUELITO goes to leave.)* On your way out, clean up the toilet--it looks like a pig sty.
CONSUELITO: Well, I haven't gone all day, so... *(She leaves.)*
LORENZO: You son-of-a-gun, you have a great wife. You ought to be happy.
CLEOFAS: Yeah, she's really nice, you're right. What can I say?
HORTENSIA: She's an idiot. God, if only you had married Antonia. She's the one who had money.
CLEOFAS: Mama, you're the one who advised me to marry Consuelito.
HORTENSIA: It was a hoax, you know? A real swindle... I feel a little dizzy... Oh, Lord. *(She opens a bottle.)* This is the time of day when they've prescribed a little shot of something for me. It reminds me of when I was a kid. Would you like some?
LORENZO: No, thanks, drink it in good health.
HORTENSIA: Her mother was a fortune teller. And some fortune teller she was, the bitch. She passed off this corpse to us making us think she had

a fortune stashed away for her. And look at her: mentally retarded and without a cent. What a lopsided marriage!
CLEOFAS: Mama, she was your in-law.
HORTENSIA: She was a damned outlaw... And this son of mine is a saint.
CLEOFAS: I like Consuelito a lot, Mama. *(At this point, CONSUELITO passes through without saying anything.)*
HORTENSIA: Well, I don't. Not even any kids, Lorenzo. She's not even capable of having kids. Something so easy you could do it in the dark. At least with a husband like this who, I tell you, is a perfect gem.
CLEOFAS: Come on, Mama. What's Lorenzo going to think?
LORENZO: Me? Nothing. I think your mother is a charmer.
HORTENSIA: Well, now, that's the way I feel about you. I'd better keep quiet. Why don't we have a game of cards with partners? It would be fascinating to exchange signals with Lorenzo...
CLEOFAS: Mama, you want to play cards here? You know that I don't like to. Why don't you knit a little sweater for the St. Vincent clothing drive.
HORTENSIA: Because I don't feel like it. And besides, I get dizzy doing such close work. Cleofás carries holiness to such an extreme that I'd be better off going to a convent. Listen, son, a convent compared to this place would be a beach resort for me. *(Her eyes moisten.)*
CLEOFAS: *(Repentive.)* It's just that I have to correct some Latin exercises.
LORENZO: And I have to put on my uniform. I'm sorry but at eight o'clock I have reserve duty. And since it's the first day...
HORTENSIA: Ah, the uniform. That was the only thing missing. I can't wait to see it. *Desideravi desideratus,* as Cleofás would say--that sounds so impressive. I think the average man on the street loses out a lot. The church and the army: those are the ones who really know what they're doing.
CLEOFAS: Do you remember the second year of Latin in the seminary?
LORENZO: I remember the second year. The Latin--I don't remember a thing.
CLEOFAS: Neither did I. I started learning it later, by correspondence... Phaedrus's fables. What lessons they teach! All of life is a fable by Phaedrus. *(CONSUELITO passes by with a cassock in her hands.)*
HORTENSIA: Where are you going?
CONSUELITO: To brush off my husband's cassock, what do you think?
HORTENSIA: What manners. Go fry the beans that were left over from lunch. I just love old clothes.

CONSUELITO: Well, your son's not too crazy about them. You ought to buy him a new cassock because this one looks like it's silverplated the way it shines so much.
HORTENSIA: You stupid idiot! If you cleaned the frosting off from your hands before you brushed it, it wouldn't shine so much.
CONSUELITO: Well, bring me some turpentine.
HORTENSIA: Sulfuric acid is what I'd bring you, you lazy slut.
CONSUELITO: *(Feeling hurt.)* Don't try to ridicule me in front of this gentleman.
CLEOFAS: That's enough now... *(He scarcely looks up from his notebooks.)*
HORTENSIA: As if somebody has to make you look ridiculous, you pipsqueak. Do us a favor...
CONSUELITO: I wish I could have died when I hit my head on that curb. I wish I could die right now. Die and have the world end at the same time.
HORTENSIA: You see? What selfishness! *(She gets up to make her leave and chases her out.)* Bring us some coffee, right now.
CLEOFAS: *(In the meantime.) Introibo ad altarem Dei.* We were going to rise to the altar of God, Lorenzo. And now, what? We'll never make it unless it's through the back door. There's a sadness there that you barely notice, but it's there, quiet, kept guarded deep inside you.
LORENZO: I've never been good at guarding anything... And now, without my even thinking about it, I'm on guard duty. Just think.
HORTENSIA: This rascal has a sense of humor!
LORENZO: You flatter me, Señora.
CLEOFAS: Look at the way this student begins his translation of the fifth fable of the first book: "An ass, in a timid field, was grazing an old man." They get everything all mixed up. Nobody studies the Classics anymore.
HORTENSIA: When it comes to that, the church is the guiltiest of them all. Now that the mass is not in Latin, they're selling themselves off at a discount...
CLEOFAS: *In hostium clamore subito territus...* You understand?
LORENZO: Not a thing, kid.
CLEOFAS: Look, man, look. "A humble old man was grazing his ass in a field. Frightened by the sudden approach of his enemies, he exhorted the ass to leave so they wouldn't get captured." The last sentence has the particle *ne.* "But the ass, without hurrying, asked him: Do you think...?" You see, at the end here, the question *Putas?*

HORTENSIA: It sounds like a filthy word to me.
CLEOFAS: Oh, come on, Mama... "Do you think the victor will make me carry two saddlepacks at a time? No, said the old man. Then, why should I worry about whom I serve if I have to carry one pack, in any case?"
HORTENSIA: That's true.
CLEOFAS: It's hard to believe you don't remember. *Nihil prater domini nomen mutant pauperes:* For poor people, the only thing that changes is their master's name." How beautiful Latin is! How beautiful Phaedrus is!
HORTENSIA: *(Ecstatically.)* How beautiful Lorenzo is!
LORENZO: *(Trying to protect himself.)* I'm going to change. Excuse me.
HORTENSIA: Oh, of course. *(She watches him leave.)*
CLEOFAS: Mama, I'd like to have a serious talk with you.
HORTENSIA: Come on, son... just because I flirted a bit with a boy who could be my grandson... Really, my grandson...
CLEOFAS: It's not that, Mama. I've got some bad news from the Bishop's Office. I wanted to tell you about it alone.
HORTENSIA: You're trying to scare me. If you want I can start on that new sweater for the poor right now, eh? It was only a joke...
CLEOFAS: No, no; listen to me. Don Remigio is getting on in years.
HORTENSIA: You're not saying that because of me.
CLEOFAS: No. I'm thinking about him.
HORTENSIA: What I mean is his age is not my fault. I keep him well fed. Of course, in spite of his being a little senile, he's got an appetite like a horse...
CLEOFAS: Yes. But he's not the issue.
HORTENSIA: And let's not even talk about you: you've relieved him of everything. He doesn't even carry one pack on his back.
CLEOFAS: It's still too much... At the Bishop's Office, they have some doubts about the administration of this parish.
HORTENSIA: They'd be better off having doubts about the administration of the Bishop's Office.
CLEOFAS: Mama, we're getting off the subject...
HORTENSIA: Keep quiet and listen. I agree that you've got to show more virtue than you have. But there's a big difference between that and not having anything to eat . A dead saint is no good for anything but to pray to.
CLEOFAS: If they heard you, Mama.

HORTENSIA: If they heard me, I would keep quiet. But they can't hear me now. Answer me: where would you be without me? You'd be a small town yokel... Or worse, a miner. And now, look at you here, with your long robe, which makes the birds happy just to see you... Hasn't life gone well for you because you let me guide you through the things of the world? Tell me, hasn't it gone well?
CLEOFAS: Yes, Mama.
HORTENSIA: Didn't I get you out of the poverty we were sunk into by your father, who you didn't even get to know? *(She makes the sign of the cross.)* May the plague eat him up if he's alive.
CLEOFAS: Yes, Mama. Look, I'm eternally...
HORTENSIA: Forget about eternities... And don't come to me later saying "Give me some moola, Abdullah." Because you tell me: What do we have, after all? Are we even bishops? Or governors? Or landlords, at least, like Don Jenaro? We're nothing. Nothing. A few appliances. And paying for them on the installment plan. Up to our ears in hock. We live like everybody else. Like all decent people: not one peseta in savings. Day to day. Day to day, and with no hope for improvement. No, son, no. My conscience doesn't bother me at all.
CLEOFAS: But, Mama, the remorse, at night... and all this mess...
HORTENSIA: For those that don't know how to survive, for those that don't know how to close their eyes at the right time, the hell with them, Cleofás. I know what it is to be hungry. When I was ten years old, the only thing I had was one céntimo buried in a hole in the backyard. Then, one night, when I was fifteen, somebody suddenly stuck fifty pesetas in my hand and something else in another place. I gritted my teeth and I said: "That's it."
CLEOFAS: I don't know what you're talking about.
HORTENSIA: Yes, you do, but it doesn't matter. That's water under the bridge... If I were a man, I would've become a priest. And when you were born, I saw a whole new world open up: a priest! No more hard work... clean, respected... socializing... With your cassock. With your maniples, with your epaulets...
CLEOFAS: Those are for admirals, Mama.
HORTENSIA: With your mink stoles.
CLEOFAS: Those are for ladies.
HORTENSIA: With your brocade chasuble... Or aren't those for priests, either?
CLEOFAS: Yes, they are... but times have changed.

HORTENSIA: You're telling me. The times and us. But we're not going to let ourselves die because of that... You couldn't become a priest... *(CLEOFAS stands to speak.)* Because you were a bit slow, I know. And the work I had to do to pay for the seminary... But here we are: now, what? I can't even make use of a few trinkets that are ridiculously rotting away in the church. Sure, let the termites swell up their bellies, and here we are with our stomachs empty... No, Cleofás. God doesn't want that.

CLEOFAS: *(To CONSUELITO, who comes in upset, with the coffees.)* What's the matter? *(CONSUELITO doesn't answer.)* You look like you're out of breath.

CONSUELITO: Yes, from brushing your cassock so much. *(CLEOFAS starts to caress her.)* Don't touch me.

HORTENSIA: What do you mean telling your husband not to touch you? He'll do what he feels like, right?

CLEOFAS: Mama! "A companion I gave you and not a servant." *Amabilio ut Rachel, sapiens ut Rebeca, longaeva et fidelus ut Sara.*

HORTENSIA: Don't give me all that ut .

CLEOFAS: It says it very clearly in the wedding ceremony.

HORTENSIA: As if the bride and groom at that point are in the mood for knowing what's said to them. They're involved in their own thing. Or in their partner's thing, which is natural. Don't worry about anything, Cleofás, because your mother is right here.

CLEOFAS: So what?

HORTENSIA: What do you mean, "so what?" Here she is. Christ, there are a lot of orphans around. Naturally, if you had a mother like some people have, you'd be better off being an orphan. *(CONSUELITO starts to cry.)*

CLEOFAS: Poor little thing, don't pay attention to her.

CONSUELITO: Have pity on me. Somebody have pity on me. I don't have anybody. I'm all alone...

HORTENSIA: Sure, on top of everything, take her side. That's all she needed to give her a leg to stand on.

CONSUELITO: Sure, you'd like me to stand up just to watch me fall down and get squelched.

HORTENSIA: My, my, what words you can learn going from carnival to carnival. *(LORENZO comes in, dressed in his uniform.)* Ah, yes... *(CONSUELITO looks at him and cries some more.)* Ah, no...

CLEOFAS: I don't understand anything.

HORTENSIA: Nor do you need to, my son. That's why you have your mother.

LORENZO: *(Conscious of the effect he is having, showing off.)* Shall I ring the Rosary bells?
HORTENSIA: You can ring my bells whenever you want, handsome. *(LORENZO goes up to the bell tower. CLEOFAS puts on his cassock. HORTENSIA caresses the cap that LORENZO has left on the table. The bells are heard. CONSUELITO stops crying and gulps a bit. Pause.)* They've been silent for so long, as if they didn't exist, and listen to them, listen to them, singing like mad. Exactly the same as my heart. *(She drinks her coffee.)*
CLEOFAS: What pleasure! What pleasure those bronze tongues give out! *Domine, labia mea aperies.*
HORTENSIA: *Et cum spiritu tuo.*
CONSUELITO: It must be glorious to hear the bells of Orleans ring. There must not be any suffering souls there. There must not be any suffering at all there. *(She sighs.)* Orleans is the top of the mountain.
HORTENSIA: Cleofás, God has visited us with this Lorenzo. He lifts up your heart.
CLEOFAS: Which means *Sursum corda. (LORENZO comes downstairs.)*
HORTENSIA: How stupid I've been! I've got an idea. Let's all get together like in those legislative sessions they write about in the newspapers. You'll see that I'm right. A coffee-drinking session.
CLEOFAS: *(Thinking of the church.)* But Mama, people are going to start to come in.
HORTENSIA: Let them wait five minutes; the Blessed Virgin is not going to run away from them. Lorenzo, handsome, you're like one of us. I'm going to treat you like a family member. It seems reasonable, since we're going to be such good friends.
LORENZO: If you like...
HORTENSIA: I like, I like. Get on my right. You be the official who stands up for us. The one we taxpayers pay to run our affairs and pick off our lice, among other things. *(To CLEOFAS.)* You, on my left. You can represent the interests of the church.
CLEOFAS: And you?
HORTENSIA: I'll represent myself, and all those who come into the session.
CONSUELITO: And me?
HORTENSIA: You be the ones who don't come in, for all your opinion is worth! You just stay there and try, as always, to look, listen and shut up. Your only job is to say yes to everything. It wouldn't be bad to have an audience that obeyed, like Pedro's ass.
CLEOFAS: It's not Pedro. It's Phaedrus.

HORTENSIA: It's all the same. *(Signaling to the men to come closer.)* I'll sit down on this trunk, which has my family mementos. I'll feel more secure. On these and between these two pillars. *(Referring to LORENZO and CLEOFAS.)* Ah, what pillars! If we've moved away from them sometimes, God only knows it's been for their own good. Uniforms are always pretty, but sometimes they're not so intelligent. I should know, since I adore them. Let's start, Cleofás. Let's hear it. That business about the Bishop's Office and all that. *(CLEOFAS starts to speak.)* Stand up. You have to give importance to things; otherwise, nobody will believe them.

CLEOFAS: *(He signals all around him.)* Before all this happened, the parish priest was more than just that; he was a pastor in the true sense of its meaning: shepherd.

HORTENSIA: Whether Don Remigio was a shepherd or an agronomy expert is not important to us now. Get to the point, get to the point.

CLEOFAS: But he was careless with his administrative duties. And he unloaded them on me. I have been... *(He looks at HORTENSIA.)* We have been the real administrators. Especially since a few months ago when he... Don Remigio is an old man. He's at an age...

HORTENSIA: *(Cutting in.)* Yes, an advanced age. What I mean is that he's ga-ga.

CLEOFAS: Then he began to show us some special kindnesses, which apparently have been misinterpreted. The bishop's intention is very clear: in no time at all he'll name a new parish priest.

HORTENSIA: That's a change that's far from good for us. Say it, say it.

LORENZO: It's not good for me either. But now I get it... Certain sales have been made, certain expropriations of superfluous ornaments...

HORTENSIA: But always with the full consent of Don Remigio, understand? When he told us yes, his mind was always very clear. He's like a ram.

CLEOFAS: A lamb, Mama.

HORTENSIA: The articles in question were always sold to go for repairing wear and tear on the building, to make our humble dwelling a little more decent.

CLEOFAS: Sure, Mama, but the dome is still caving in.

HORTENSIA: That's because the centuries don't go by without having some effect. For example, Don Remigio himself, who's not quite a century old yet and who's very kind, has gone to pot. My father was a landowner and he always used to say: "A parish lasts longer than a parish priest, an olive grove lasts longer than a cabinet minister." Because nothing lasts

forever, Cleofás, no matter what you do. Didn't they teach you that in the seminary?
CONSUELITO: I've had enough!
CLEOFAS: Mama, we have to replace what was stolen.
HORTENSIA: You mean what was borrowed.
CLEOFAS: For example, the painting that you sent out to be restored three months ago. The candle holders in the sanctuary, which you said had to be regilded...
HORTENSIA: It's not my fault if the restorers and the gilders go off to Germany and the ones that are left are unreliable. Forget about all these details. Damned Bishop's Office.
CLEOFAS: Mama, but where did all these appliances come from?
HORTENSIA: From our efforts. Nowadays everybody has them. The standard of living. Or don't you read the newspapers? Peace and washing machines; that's our motto.
CLEOFAS: People are talking, Mama. They're saying things in the streets, in the bars, in the shops, during the breaks at the movies.
HORTENSIA: About wha...a...at?
CLEOFAS: They're saying that we're feeding on the parish. That we came in here starving and we've turned purple from the feast we've been having.
HORTENSIA: Maybe they're thinking about the purple altar during the Advent feast.
CLEOFAS: They're saying that we're skimming off everything in sight. That we're selling the candles, that we're emptying out the collection plate of San Pancracio...
HORTENSIA: Well, those that are talking would be better off keeping quiet because everybody's taken a slice out of the church. It's just that some piss in a pot and others piss on a pillow. I've kept quite a few mouths shut with tinsel from the altars. You're better off not listening to that garbage.
CLEOFAS: Doña Rufa, Soledad the corporal's wife, Remedios down at the milk market, everybody... they're wondering if Don Remigio is a puppet in our hands, if you've got him by the...
HORTENSIA: *(Jumping up.)* See, that's just cheap low-class spite.
CLEOFAS: We have to get money... get back the paintings, the candelabras, the silver parish cross with its cloth covering. Everything, Mama. The church has been dismantled.
HORTENSIA: That's been happening for centuries. The way you're talking you'd think we only came in here to plunder.

CLEOFAS: Don't make me nervous. In a month Don Remigio will either be dead or retired. I'm responsible for everything. There's an inventory. They have a copy in the Bishop's Office. For God's sake, Mama, what are we going to do? What are we going to do?
HORTENSIA: You're getting hysterical, Cleofás! You've never been like that. But why do we have this uniform on our side? What do you think, my brave officer?
LORENZO: There's an old Chinese proverb that says: There are thirty-six ways of escaping from danger but the best of all is to start running. You can ask for a transfer to another parish before the change takes place.
CLEOFAS: Run away?
HORTENSIA: That's the typical opinion of an authority!... We wouldn't be able to go away far enough. And we would have to make some gifts... to blur some memories... We're not ready for that yet.
CLEOFAS: Money, money, money, money...
HORTENSIA: Do me the favor of not being so mercenary and attached to worldly goods. It doesn't become you. You leave that to me. Besides, everything is taken care of! Didn't you read this letter from America? Your Uncle Sebi is deathly ill. What kind of shape can he be in if a nun from the clinic had to write the letter for him? And he remembers me in his hour of death. Because he's ready to kick the bucket. God, in his infinite mercy, will gather up my cousin Sebi from this life before he takes Don Remigio. I've got an eye when it comes to deaths.
CONSUELITO: Well, then you should have become a doctor.
HORTENSIA: Quiet, birdbrain!... Luck is knocking at our door. An uncle in America, Cleofás: the dream of thirty-one million Spaniards. And he's probably dying right now, thanks be to God, naturally.
CLEOFAS: *Requiem aeternam dona eis, domine.*
HORTENSIA: *Et lux perpetuam luceat ei.* What a fun afternoon you're having, my boy... In the meantime, we'll do what we've always done: buy raffle tickets from the blind vendors, enter the football pools, play the lottery...
CONSUELITO: Go to the bullfights...
CLEOFAS: No, no, no. We've been living lies for so many years that even we don't believe ourselves any more. We've got to return the parish to the original state we found it in. No more illusions. No more unholy miracles. We've got to put our feet down on solid ground. Let's be realistic: the first thing is to make a novena to Santa Rita, patron of the hopeless...
LORENZO: Or a triduum to San Antonio, patron of lost objects.

CONSUELITO: *(Stepping up on her chair.)*

> If it's miracles you seek,
> Behold death and error afield,
> With demons and misery gone,
> The sick and the lepers healed.

HORTENSIA: Don't give me all that crap.
CONSUELITO: *(As if in ecstacy.)*

> The danger now subsides.
> The poor get a helping hand.
> Let pilgrims and Paduans spread
> The word throughout the land.

HORTENSIA: *(To CLEOFAS.)* You're the one who understands her; shut her up.
CONSUELITO: *(Completely carried away now.)*

> Ah, sweet tomb of mine,
> Away from my thoughts, long gone.
> And so many lay down to sleep
> Who are discovered dead at the dawn.

HORTENSIA: Shut her up or I won't be held responsible.

CONSUELITO:

> I acknowledge all of my faults
> And my sins are humbly confessed.
> Grant me the sacraments, please;
> Reach out and let me be blessed.

HORTENSIA: Call out the Civil Guard and have them shoot her...

CONSUELITO:

> San Antonio and Santa Rita,
> All is resplendent about you.
> Thanks be to God, thanks be to God.

(With great naturalness.) I got it all out! *(She gets down from her chair.)* It's the extra special prayer my mother used to recite when she was missing something. *(During the above invocations of CONSUELITO, LORENZO had not stopped laughing, while CLEOFAS devoted himself to praying along, both actions taking place until the final words of CONSUELITO: "I got it all out!" Now there is absolute silence.)*

HORTENSIA: Well, then again, your mother was some crappy fortune teller. Keep quiet, you creep, and frost some stars.
CONSUELITO: Wait! I just got an idea from the saints. And we can get going on this right away...
HORTENSIA: She's at it again! God, she's at it again...
CONSUELITO: A raffle. We've got to have a street raffle for charity.
HORTENSIA: Oh, the fool. Those that say that God speaks through the mouths of the simple-minded are right. What nonsense!... But what a good idea!
CLEOFAS: Have you lost your mind?
HORTENSIA: A raffle, while we're waiting for the inheritance papers from my cousin in America...
CLEOFAS: But what will we raffle off?
HORTENSIA: Everything. Anything. The few gilded ornaments left in the church, a couple of dolls, some trash baskets. *(Getting excited.)* With one altar skirt we can make a couple of beautiful table cloths. Besides, we'll put the crazy wardrobe ladies to work, which is what they want. This'll be a terrific business deal. *(A loud noise is heard in the church.)* Some pious old lady must be getting impatient.
CLEOFAS: I don't know. You've convinced me. You always convince me. Let's hope it all turns out all right. *(He leaves. Soon, the sound of prayers is heard.)*
HORTENSIA: *(To CONSUELITO.)* You, go do your thing. And don't think that just because you had one idea in your life that that's going to set you free. *(CONSUELITO exits. To LORENZO.)* I think you go along with me in everything, right? In everything. And since you're the one who's supposed to keep order, you'll take charge, isn't that so?
LORENZO: Yes, Señora, why shouldn't I?
HORTENSIA: In front of Cleofás, certain things can't be said, but you're more human. I've got stashed away a few door panels, a few altarpieces...

LORENZO: A few bells, because there are six of them and how many do we need?... I like being a bell ringer but not that much, not that much...
HORTENSIA: Ah, I needed a man to come and go, to give me strength. I'm just so feminine... *(With another tone.)* And I know antique dealers. *(Same tone as before.)* See you later, Lorenzo, my little accomplice.
LORENZO: Good-by, Doña Hortensia.
HORTENSIA: *(Putting on a veil.)* Doña? You wouldn't call a flower by it's formal name, would you? Call me Hortensia, plain and simple.
LORENZO: Are you just a plain simple flower?
HORTENSIA: Ah, you can see why I've always gotten along so well with the last man to come along. *(She exits, laughing, through the church door. Immediately afterward CONSUELITO enters with her eyes downcast.)*
LORENZO: Consuelito, why didn't you want to speak to me inside there before? *(He lifts up her chin.)*
CONSUELITO: Why did you come?
LORENZO: You're not happy here.
CONSUELITO: I was before, when I used to go around from town to town, doing somersaults like a monkey. Without anybody telling me: "Sit down, shut up, scrub that toilet." But I was getting used to not being any happier. And then you come along and look at me and all the while I keep hearing bells without knowing where they come from.
LORENZO: They're from Orleans... I love you, Consuelito.
CONSUELITO: Sure. In a pig's eye. You're some artist.
LORENZO: You are, too. They're not.
CONSUELITO: Neither am I. I'm sore from this morning's somersaults... Your joints get out of shape fast. Why don't you leave and let us be the way we were and don't stop until you get to Orleans; don't do what I did...
LORENZO: You can help me.
CONSUELITO: How?
LORENZO: When the time comes, I'll let you know...
CONSUELITO: At your service. You'll soon be happy. I can read the future: more so than my mother, I think.
LORENZO: Speak into my ear so we won't distract the people saying the rosary.
CONSUELITO: I said that you'll get to ring the bells in Orleans. And when people get what they want, they get everything at the same time.
LORENZO: And you? What would you like to get for yourself? How can I get you?

CONSUELITO: Me? *(He starts to kiss her, taking advantage of her speaking into his ear.)* Lorenzo, what are you doing? I'm married. Very badly, but I'm married... Lorenzo. Your belt is sticking me, man... *(She is referring to his uniform.)*
LORENZO: Consuelito... Come with me to Orleans. *(She sighs, letting herself go.)*
CONSUELITO: Orleans? God! Oh, God! What a fool I am. *(He murmurs "Fool, fool, fool," as he kisses her.)* I'm lost... But, what can I do if I'm a fool? Oh, what happiness. *(Prayers are heard and there is a...*

SLOW CURTAIN

ACT TWO

SCENE I

It is nighttime. LORENZO is seated in the barber's chair. CLEOFAS prepares the necessary things to shave him, which he does, at least partially, during the following dialog. From time to time, taking advantage of the fact that CLEOFAS has his back to her, CONSUELITO appears through the door to the street. She is dressed in an exotic Middle Eastern costume, capped by an enormous purple turban. She makes appearances to throw piles of passionate kisses to LORENZO.

LORENZO: Who the hell got you interested in barbering? Because, when it comes to making a decision, you never do.
CLEOFAS: Not me or anybody else. Life is the one that decides. Do you remember how we would dream in that seminary room? You, about ringing the morning bells in Orleans. Me, in converting pagans. I didn't know what I wanted to convert them to or from. I just wanted to convert them.
LORENZO: Our job has always been to convert pagans or to kill them.
CLEOFAS: We would dream...
LORENZO: Well, they woke me up with a jolt: they kicked me out...
CLEOFAS: Man...
LORENZO: I wanted to leave, but they kicked me out. They caught me sending messages to all the seminarians' sisters... I had thirteen girl friends. When we passed by in line it was a riot. They used to wave at me from the balconies. I was always hot for action and they kicked me out; that's normal. But you were kind of a nerd. What happened to you?
CLEOFAS: Time caught up to me. The new kids that came in passed me by. If I was promoted from one semester to the next it was only because there wasn't room for me in the classes. I was always pretty dumb. *(An appearance by CONSUELITO.)* They finally wound up calling me "The Old War Horse"... In order not to be a burden, in order for them to take pity on me--which is the only thing I've known how to do well--I used to help out in the barber shop. And I wound up learning the trade.
LORENZO: In other words, they kicked you out, too?
CLEOFAS: You don't kick an ashtray out of a house. And that's what I was... They wouldn't have kicked me out. But one day, my mother came... God, Lorenzo, what a mother! *(LORENZO moves because, once again, CONSUELITO has appeared.)* Is it too hot?
LORENZO: No, go ahead; I just got a little cramp here.

CLEOFAS: Then, my mother came... She ran a boarding house...
LORENZO: Was it public housing for old folks?
CLEOFAS: No, it was a private house for young ladies.
LORENZO: Ah, yes. *(He laughs.)*
CLEOFAS: I don't know why, but they made her close it down. It was in fifty-six.
LORENZO: In the month of March?
CLEOFAS: Yeah, around Holy Week... She came and she got me out of there. She didn't want to go on living alone; she was past her prime for working...
LORENZO: Sure, she was past her prime. Just think.
CLEOFAS: And she had already given up the idea of having a priest as a son. But she didn't want a barber either. She made me compete for a job in the Department of Public Works. But by that time my brain wasn't up to it. In any case, since she knows a lot of people, I got to be the sexton here.
LORENZO: The thing you've always liked to do is to put your head under your wing and let others live your life for you, isn't that so? Well, that's your problem...
CLEOFAS: Like guys that wanted to be bullfighters... and are now bullfighters' aides. Or worse yet, picador's aides.
LORENZO: But you have your compensations...
CLEOFAS: *(In a vague way.)* Maybe I do. Maybe I'm playing the martyr. Because my life couldn't end any other way. They wouldn't bring me the Nobel Prize here at the sacristy... But you can't even say I'm a failure. A failure is somebody who's tried something which didn't turn out for him. I haven't tried anything. The only thing I've done is to go along with everybody. Of course, I do have Consuelito.
LORENZO: Do you love her a lot?
CLEOFAS: She's the only thing I have. *(An appearance by CONSUELITO. She blows kisses again.)*
LORENZO: You also have your mother.
CLEOFAS: No, she's the one who has me. She doesn't realize it but deep down that's what it is. Consuelito is just like me: simple minded. Her name is Consuelo and that's just what she is: my consolation. *(Seriously.)* What I like is to see her frosting the stars, while I'm cleaning up the altar gilding. She's just like a little bird.
LORENZO: But haven't you all clipped her wings?
CLEOFAS: No... she's so used to her cage, that even if the door were opened, she wouldn't fly away. That's for sure.

LORENZO: Does she know you love her?
CLEOFAS: Yes, I told her one day, when I proposed.
LORENZO: Did you tell her, or did your mother do it?
CLEOFAS: I don't even remember. But she knows.
LORENZO: And haven't you ever told her again?
CLEOFAS: What for? We're not what you would call passionate lovers...
LORENZO: But, man, just to tell her you love her at least once a month...
CLEOFAS: It just wouldn't go over very well for the two of us to talk about love. We'd probably start laughing. Love is for other people; for important people who have lots of free time. We've got enough on our hands just to keep living together.
LORENZO: But for a woman, that's boring... and dangerous.
CLEOFAS: I don't understand women very well. You can imagine how the ones that deal with sextons are: straightlaced, more or less.
LORENZO: Excuse me for butting into your affairs but, I mean, at night...
CLEOFAS: Usually, we're very tired. And when we're not, you know: that stuff doesn't last very long...
LORENZO: Maybe for you, since you're not too hot to trot...
CLEOFAS: Besides, since we don't talk about it the next morning... it's as if nothing happened. *(Acting slyly.)* Don't think that in the beginning we didn't do any winking and hugging and grabbing and things like that. Until one day my mother told us she was tired of witnessing filthy behavior. *(Eleven o'clock strikes on the church clock.)* And now, this change in the parish is making me lose sleep. God only knows if we'll be out in the street like a bunch of wandering minstrels...
LORENZO: You've got to have some confidence, Cleofás.
CLEOFAS: Yeah. And a clean conscience. I've agreed to too much. I've been weak: *timor reventialis* more than anything... *(The voice of DON REMIGIO is heard.)*
VOICE OF DON REMIGIO: My fellow parishioners: Adam is the one that ate the apple, but it backfired on all of us. What a mess it made!
CLEOFAS: There goes Don Remigio. As soon as he hears eleven o'clock ring, he thinks it's in the morning and he starts preaching as if it were high mass. Wait until I take him home, okay?... *(He exits through the church door.)*
VOICE OF DON REMIGIO: God is good. Yes, yes. God is good but not foolish. And the day He gets fed up, you'll see. You wanted to keep Him locked up in your closet. Very well. He'll explode on you in there. And damn it, I'll be happy. *(CONSUELITO runs in, hugs LORENZO, who is half shaved, and gets herself covered with soap.)*

LORENZO: Please, woman, please.
CLEOFAS: *(In the background, offstage.)* Come down from the pulpit, Don Remigio. It's nighttime and there's nobody here. Let's go to bed; we've got to get some rest.
VOICE OF DON REMIGIO: What do you mean "go to bed?" It's my duty to preach the word of God, whether anyone hears me or not.
CLEOFAS: *(From within.)* Be a good fellow. Come on, I'll go with you.
LORENZO: Please!
CONSUELITO: Are we going to see each other when they go to bed?
LORENZO: Yes, that's why I told your husband to shave me, in order not to scrape your face. But the way you're diving all over me... As if I were a swimming pool.
CONSUELITO: I love you, I love you, I love you.
LORENZO: Again? *(She appears to be sick to her stomach.)* That's some bath you're giving your stomach.
CONSUELITO: It's not because of the soap. Afterwards, I'll let you in on a little secret.
LORENZO: How about a hint, my little harem girl?
CONSUELITO: You shouldn't be making fun of me just because I happen to love you...
LORENZO: I'm not making fun of you. It's just that you look so...
CONSUELITO: What do you think, I'm not so comfortable with this outfit, either. The turban is fine because it was my mother's. But not this outfit. It was on one of those saints on the Easter floats and I feel kind of strange wearing it... now... with our relationship. Of course, dressed up like this, I'm a walking ad. I attract a lot of people to the raffle. Mostly, just to look.
LORENZO: It doesn't surprise me.
CONSUELITO: Because when it comes to playing, they almost never do. This is what I was able to swipe today. Here, take it. *(She gives him a handful of coins.)*
LORENZO: Everything in loose change?
CONSUELITO: Well, Doña Hortensia grabs all the bills... When are we leaving for Orleans, Lorenzo? *(He counts the money.)* I don't like living like I do, without knowing who I belong to. It doesn't go with my personality. I don't think I'm very good at playing around.
LORENZO: *(Putting away the money.)* We still don't have enough.
CONSUELITO: Well, let's go on foot. I could do some acts in the towns while you pass the hat. Tell me about Orleans.
LORENZO: I already told you all I know.

CONSUELITO: Does it have lots of towers or only one big one?
LORENZO: It has one big one, full of bells.
CONSUELITO: *(Hinting.)* And storks. *(She embraces him.)*
LORENZO: You never get enough, do you?
CONSUELITO: I never get enough, you beautiful creature; you've got me crazy. Let's leave for Orleans right now. *(She pulls him.)*
LORENZO: At least wait until I get the other half of my face shaved, all right? And let's save a little more money and get our papers in order... Aren't you happy here with me?
CONSUELITO: Yes, but I need to tell everybody that I love you. I don't want to love you on the sly like a fruit snatcher.
LORENZO: *(Whose thoughts have been elsewhere.)* What does your mother-in-law have in that trunk?
CONSUELITO: Don't mention her name. She's a pig. Don't you think I know she's got her eye on you?
LORENZO: We could pick the lock... If there were anything valuable in it, we could leave earlier for Orleans.
CONSUELITO: He doesn't love her! How great! He doesn't love her! Tonight, after we finish, we'll open it up. *(Embracing him.)* Oh, God!
HORTENSIA: *(Coming in from the street.)* What are you doing here? You go out again for a while. My feet are killing me... Where's Cleofás?
LORENZO: He'll be right back. He was shaving me...
HORTENSIA: *(Suspicious.)* I can see. And what about you? Were you washing your face?
CONSUELITO: Yes; I washed up because I was hot.
HORTENSIA: And you still are, you hot little thing. But get all the soap off. *(With all her strength, she wipes a towel across her face.)*
CONSUELITO: Ow, ow!
HORTENSIA: When I start pulling the covers off this thing and find out what's going on...
CONSUELITO: *(Challenging her.)* You'll find out that you're the one that's not underneath the covers.
HORTENSIA: Get out there! They're stealing the prizes, you slut. *(CONSUELITO leaves.)* That bitch is going to make me lose faith. And you, you've been sticking to her tighter than somebody that's been sticking it to her.
LORENZO: Me?
HORTENSIA: Sure, put on a surprised look under all that whipped cream. I'm warning you, when I'm bad, I'm very bad; but when I'm good I'm worse. And you're pushing me over the edge. For three months you've

been avoiding me but I can't control myself anymore... *(She comes on to him.)* It's time for me to scramble for a piece of the action...

(It must be said that neither now nor later should it be assumed that HORTENSIA is in love with LORENZO. HORTENSIA knows what is going on with everything, including herself. She jokes, she laughs. If she can get something out of all the joking, she does. If not, so be it. LORENZO also jokes around at times. At other times he doesn't, because he's afraid.)

Don't waste your time with my mousy daughter-in-law, Lorenzo: I'm telling you for your own good. You've got the pharmacist's wife, who's still got a nice set of boobs; and Doña Catalina, so pleasantly plump... and they're always ready to give you a few coins for playing around a bit.

LORENZO: Señora...

HORTENSIA: Without exaggerating... Just think of the profits we could make from that flesh and this mouth...

LORENZO: Watch out, your son's coming back.

HORTENSIA: *(Speaking through her laughter.)* Let him. Or doesn't he know how I became his mother? Did I get pregnant with an *ora pro nobis?* Ah, Lorenzo, I've never seen anybody with such hot blood as yours in my life. Here's half of what I took in today from the raffle. Take it. *(She gives him an envelope.)*

LORENZO: That's not bad for now.

HORTENSIA: I swear... That was some idea that tricky bitch had... And you've still got your wandering eye, without trying to capitalize on your talents, the way God commands... What a waste!

LORENZO: Don't I go to bed with whoever you tell me to?

HORTENSIA: Yes, but without conviction, with too much reserve... The thing is, you're not cut out to be a pimp or anything like that... God, with your body and my brains, we could go places... Anyway, we'll see what happens. Let's see if poverty softens your heart. Because otherwise... Without any news about my American cousin. Without any news from the Department of Public Works, and I wrote to Don Fulgencio a month ago...

LORENZO: But, Doña Hortensia, do you think that'll work out?

HORTENSIA: Shit, don't call me Doña. Why shouldn't it work out? I've got some pull there. Don Fulgencio is the director. He couldn't find a spot for Cleofás because Cleofás would compose prayers on the inventory

lists, but you're different. Ah, I'll be your woman till death do us part. Lord, I'll be property surrendered to you in perpetuity. How great it'll be to leave this cloister and set up an apartment the way it's supposed to be...
LORENZO: Say, Doña Hortensia, what a classy lady you've turned into.
HORTENSIA: Don't call me Doña, Lorenzo. Or I'll eat you alive. God, what madness!
CLEOFAS: *(Entering amidst the madness.)* The poor man doesn't want to go to bed. He wants to know why he has to preach on a schedule as if it were the evening news. He preaches when he pleases. The man is incompetent now. He won't last the month.
HORTENSIA: Everybody gets what's coming to them.
CLEOFAS: Mama.
HORTENSIA: Wha... a... a... t?
CLEOFAS: Nothing. Only that that's what they must be thinking about us. We'll wind up as prisoners. In the jails of the Inquisition. And excommunicated.
HORTENSIA: Jesus, what a pain.
CLEOFAS: I found this note in the church. They must have slipped it under the door.
HORTENSIA: *(Anticipating what is coming up.)* Well, as far as I'm concerned, the place where I slip those anonymous notes is under my foot. One came in this morning. A copy of an accusation against us to the Bishop. Accusing us. Of what? What I say is they're jealous...
CLEOFAS: Finally! That accusation finally came. I knew it would turn out that way...
HORTENSIA: They're acting as though they want to spread the word to the Pope. This is like being under the sword of Demosthenes!
CLEOFAS: That's Damocles, Mama.
HORTENSIA: It's all the same.
LORENZO: *(Pointing to the paper.)* What does it say?
CLEOFAS: It looks like a poem or something like that. *(He reads.)*

"The sexton's wife is a hotcake.
The bell ringer is honey, indeed.
We've got ourselves a lumbering ox.
A she-mule is all that we need."

We've got ourselves a lumbering ox. A she-mule is all that we need. I don't know what they're talking about.

HORTENSIA: *(On purpose.)* Neither do I. And you, Lorenzo?
LORENZO: I don't know. Me? Honey?
CLEOFAS: Honey on top of hotcakes, right?... I don't know...
HORTENSIA: Everything will be cleared up tonight.
CLEOFAS: I wonder what music they play that to...
HORTENSIA: To the tune of the Royal March. Jesus, what a neighborhood! What gossip! I wish I could keep them all out of sight.
CLEOFAS: If God doesn't fix things up for us, they really will be out of sight. And in the worst way. Because with the shape Don Remigio is in... *(He goes on shaving LORENZO.)*
HORTENSIA: God, son, you just don't let go, do you? All day long worrying about the change in the parish priest. Everything's always a big crisis for you. The world's not going to end because of a new parish priest. And he won't be so new that we can't find some way how to get to him. I've known quite a few in my life.
CLEOFAS: It couldn't be to the tune of the Royal March: it just doesn't go.
HORTENSIA: Then why don't you try it to the tune of the National Anthem? Or maybe the Wildcat Strut, which might go even better. *(She hums.)* This is some time of day to be getting a shave...
LORENZO: I'm on night duty and I have to pass in review at City Hall.
HORTENSIA: What time are you coming back?
LORENZO: At six.
HORTENSIA: Well, call me because I've got a lot to do. And don't eat breakfast out. We'll have it together. *(Toward the outside.)* Consuelito! *(To CLEOFAS.)* Both of you, go to bed; you must have had a very tiring day. I'll stay with the raffle a little while longer... There's never any rest with the sanctuary... With the nice weather it seems that those slobs stay out a lot later. *(Referring to the bottle.)* I'll take this with me in case it gets cooler or in case I have to invite somebody to have a drink. You've got to understand these business dealings. *(In a lower voice to CONSUELITO, who enters.)* So then, the sexton's wife is a hotcake, eh? *(She pinches CONSUELITO.)*
CONSUELITO: You see? She's starting again.
HORTENSIA: It wasn't intentional. *(In a lower voice.)* I'll give you hotcakes, you tramp... How come you sell so few tickets for the raffle? For the whole day you haven't taken in more than twenty-seven pesetas and fifty céntimos.
CONSUELITO: Well, I've taken in more than you; you only sold twenty-five pesetas worth.
HORTENSIA: But I'm not dressed up like "The Arabian Nights."

CONSUELITO: It would be better not to talk about nights, Doña Hortensia: mine have been very profitable.
HORTENSIA: You trash! *(She exits.)*
CLEOFAS: You two don't get along very well at all.
CONSUELITO: How we get along is not up to me. She's the one that's always trying to get on my wrong side.
CLEOFAS: Lately you haven't needed anybody to get on your wrong side.
CONSUELITO: Because before, you all had me psyched out... between you and your mother... and the neighborhood kids, who are a bunch of hoodlums. But as far as things are concerned now, I have confidence in my own worth, because...
CLEOFAS: *(In reference to her clothes.)* Go on, go make yourself... normal. It's getting pretty late.
CONSUELITO: Good night, Lorenzo. And happy policing. *(She leaves for her room.)*
CLEOFAS: Holy Mother, the two of them are really out of it. They don't know how serious things are. They're like two little kids.
LORENZO: Yes, but two little kids who know a lot for their age.
CLEOFAS: Without realizing what our situation is like. Two steps away from jail, and look: insulting each other without knowing why.
LORENZO: Well, they must know.
CLEOFAS: What must they know? Whims, impulses, like two little kids. If it weren't for me... and you, naturally..
LORENZO: That's certainly true. *(He gets up and rinses off.)*
CLEOFAS: Anyway, Lorenzo, I'll see you tomorrow. I'm happy to have such a faithful friend in the house.
LORENZO: It's nothing, man. If you need a favor, all you have to do is ask. And rest up, since you're the one that can.
CLEOFAS: I can? Yes, yes...
LORENZO: Because, as far as I'm concerned... *(Purposely.)* This is going to be some night.
CLEOFAS: Just because you've got that uniform on, try not to be too tough on people who start acting up tonight. All of us in this world are good, don't you think? What happens is that we don't have a very clear idea of what we want.
LORENZO: There are those that do.
CLEOFAS: Good night, Lorenzo. *(He exits.)*
HORTENSIA: *(Who has been eavesdropping and now enters.)* Ah, what a body! Ah, what an everything, Lord.
LORENZO: Ah, what an asshole. *(Making gestures referring to CLEOFAS.)*

HORTENSIA: *(Speaking loudly.)* There was nobody around so I closed up. *(Loudly, so that LORENZO might hear her.)* My stomach is ruined from too many snacks. I could really go for a big plate of stew. *(She embraces him.)*
LORENZO: If I don't get there, the sergeant will let me have it.
HORTENSIA: Take the key and come back as soon as you can. *(She gives it to him. He starts to exit, almost fleeing.)* God, what a cold way to say good-by to someone who loves him so much.
LORENZO: I can't forget that you're the mother of a friend.
HORTENSIA: All the more reason to do me favors. When you get back you'll stop being such a prude. *(LORENZO manages to get away and leaves. HORTENSIA is a little drunk.)* He doesn't like me. He doesn't like me... Yes, he likes me but he's afraid to make a move. But I'll show you a thing or two about being afraid to act. Too many years have gone by without any stomping around, without any strutting around, without any screwing around, God! *(HORTENSIA opens up the trunk with a key. Speaking to the bottle:)* Give me some confidence, old friend; we all belong to the same club... *(In front of the trunk.)* How beautiful! How shiny! *(With a vial.)* The perfume... it's evaporated. A perfume that's driven so many heads crazy... That's a bad sign. No, no. What drives people crazy is passion, Hortensia, not perfume... *(She goes to the barber's shelf.)* Here's some cologne... Aged. *(She smells it and puts it back.)* It's so aged it makes you throw up. This one... This one is smoother. A little bit under the arms... On the neckline... Oh, baby, how refreshing!... You'd better watch out for me now, Lorenzo. We'll see who comes out on top.

(She leaves, taking some clothes to her room. As soon as HORTENSIA disappears, CONSUELITO comes out of her room, sees the trunk open, looks into it briefly, and goes into the bathroom. Immediately after, LORENZO enters and walks across toward the bell tower. Finally, it is CLEOFAS's turn: when he closes his bedroom door CONSUELITO comes out of the bathroom and goes back to the bedroom. Then LORENZO comes down with a medium-sized bell which he carries with some effort. He puts it down on the floor. From his pocket he takes out a small crowbar and a hammer. He approaches DOÑA LEONOR'S tomb and begins to loosen the hinges. Cautiously, HORTENSIA appears, dressed up as a lady of the evening from the 1930's, carrying a cigarette holder, and acting a little tipsy. When she reaches LORENZO, she taps

him on the shoulder. He turns around, frightened, probably because of the tomb.)

I'm Doña Leonor, the founder.
LORENZO: Jesus, Mary and Joseph.
HORTENSIA: What's up, sweetheart?
LORENZO: Ah, but is that you?
HORTENSIA: You're here again?
LORENZO: I left my cap.
HORTENSIA: *(Whacking the bell.)* That's some strange cap the cops are wearing now... *(To calm LORENZO, who has something to fear and knows it.)* You men can come up with some clever excuses to come falling into our arms... *(She extends them.)* Is it all right with you if we go halves on the bell? *(Without waiting for an answer.)* Make up your mind; they're falling asleep on me. *(She is referring to her arms.)* What were you doing , my fickle friend? Asking for Doña Leonor's white hand?
LORENZO: No. I... was just looking around.
HORTENSIA: Well, no wonder I used to see some mortar removed whenever I came at night to remove it myself... "What helpful rats," I thought. "Nice little rats!" If I had a son like you, I'd be the queen of Spain right now... That is, unless you cut my head off first. The hope of my old age and here you come, with your hands washed, to take away the rings.
LORENZO: But weren't you also hustling the tomb?
HORTENSIA: Here I am, giving you a commission on everything I take in and you're making deals *(She points to the tomb and the bell.)* behind my back.
LORENZO: Listen, don't the pharmacist's wife and Genoveva and Dolores give you a piece of the action when I'm the one that works?
HORTENSIA: I'm the one who gets them for you. If it wasn't for me, who delivers them to you on a silver platter... *(She sits down. He goes to do likewise.)* Go ahead, you grave robber. Let's rid Doña Leonor of all her encumbrances; that way the poor thing will be better disposed to wait for her resurrection... *(Half dreamily, half shamefully. In the meantime, LORENZO works on the gravestone.)* I've got a story, too, like she does. I started out being Horty. My summers at the beach in San Sebastian, my cherry liqueurs, my satin gowns. Everything went down the tube in a hurry. The war left us all with our feet dangling. And it was a civil war; imagine if it was a military war... At that time they called me "the

Franchise." There wasn't anything I didn't get into. We even smuggled goods in from Gibraltar, which, as far as I'm concerned the British can keep; I can't stand the place... But anyway... Around 1950 my name was "Hortensia, the Antibiotic"... Later I was "Madame Hortense," with my house of girls. Shhh, don't make noise.
LORENZO: Cleofás told me you had a boarding house for young ladies. *(Laughing.)*
HORTENSIA: He didn't tell you I was an Ursaline nun, because he doesn't have any imagination. Who could that jerk have taken after?
LORENZO: *(Laughing.)* It must have been his father.
HORTENSIA: Of course it was his father. That's why I wonder who he took after... The house wasn't going too badly. That is, up until that merciless decision by the Justice Department, which tried to make decent people out of all of us. What a disaster!... I lost my zest for life. *(In this scene the sound track of a "western" coming from the next-door movie house is heard.)* Damn, now we've got to listen to all the racket these movie people are making. Just when you're ready to go to sleep, they start emptying a machine gun into your head. They must love all that killing... *(After another drink, the narration goes on.)* Anyway, then I turned into this: into Doña Hortensia. But I was more than fed up with it, I swear to you. And then you came along, right in the middle of winter... And I stood up again with youth. Stood right up, like that dead woman... Have a drink with me. *(She approaches him.)* A life without this stinking incense: that's all I ask for.
LORENZO: *(Referring to the gravestone.)* I've got it, Doña Hortensia. Give me a hand. Here... on the gravestone... Let's go. One... two... three. *(Pause. They manage to shove aside the gravestone, after which a mummy without a casket falls out. LORENZO lets the gravestone and the body fall.)*
HORTENSIA: *(We don't know if she is serious or not.)* God, I thought it was grabbing me... what a scare! What's the matter? What do you see?
LORENZO: Nothing.
HORTENSIA: *(Bending over.)* Wow, the Countess has fallen apart; that's a hell of a way to wind up. It's because a lot of years have gone by... Where are the necklaces?
LORENZO: The only thing here is some dust and the cord from a nun's habit.
HORTENSIA: That's the way everything was: jewelry on the outside and rot on the inside. This dust came from all that mud... And what are we going to do with all this crap?

LORENZO: The bones could be sold as holy relics.
HORTENSIA: Nobody wants that stuff anymore. The headstone, yes... I'll talk to Don Juanito, the gay antique dealer. He's got a goddamn house like a sacristy... Get the corpse out of the way....
LORENZO: *(As he does so, he leans over to pick something up. It is a book, and a sheet of paper has fallen out of it.)* There's a book here. And a sheet of paper... with a poem.
HORTENSIA: Just when we're in the mood for poetry.
LORENZO: *(Reading.)*

> Unhappy death in Portugal
> Hoists up your castles here.
> Columbus let loose the Gothic tribes
> In the hidden siege of this sphere
>
> And in many ways, Oh Spain!,
> What is much easier and true
> Is that, what you alone took from all,
> All can now take back from you.

HORTENSIA: As if we could take anything away from you, gorgeous: you stupid corpse... On top of everything else, you threaten us. What a crappy countess... Get back in there again, Leonor Carrillo, you good-for-nothing trash. Wait until they call for you. *(They raise up the gravestone. A pause.)* All that work for nothing. You get to the end of your life and you've got nothing to show for it. Hold me, I'm getting the shakes. *(LORENZO takes hold of her with a hand on her shoulder.)* Don't you have a better place to put your hand? Say, this is what I call living--not those church celebrations... Death makes me high.
LORENZO: So does the booze.
HORTENSIA: I haven't drunk anything. *(Inviting him to kiss her.)* Can't you see I've got my eyes closed? *(She laughs.)* For you it's nothing but for me it means a lot... *(With her eyes closed.)* Ah, I feel something coming on! I feel something coming on! *(CONSUELITO appears in the doorway. She throws a slipper at HORTENSIA.)*
CONSUELITO: There it is!
HORTENSIA: *(She opens her eyes. Faking very badly:)* I'm a sleepwalker. Can't you see? A genuine sleepwalker... *(Referring to her outfit.)* And this is my nightgown...

CONSUELITO: Well, it's a pretty weird nightgown. It looks just like a whore's outfit that's seen its days.
HORTENSIA: *(Not faking anymore.)* What are you doing here? You pig! You jealous bitch! I'm going to tell your husband everything. Lorenzo, get her out of our bedroom. I'm free, you understand? A widow all my life. Free to come and go and to sleep with whoever I want...
CONSUELITO: If they let you. That's none of my business. I came in here to throw up, which is the best thing you can do in this house. *(As she passes by, she covers the canary's cage with a cloth.)* Don't look, Tarsi. *(She goes into the bathroom.)*
HORTENSIA: Defend me, Lorenzo. I've been dishonored. You say something to her; I'm a bit rusty at it: I used to have such a sharp tongue that people were afraid to hear me. Say something. *(HORTENSIA falls on LORENZO, but he moves back and she hits her side against the divan.)* Ow...!
LORENZO: Did you get hurt?
HORTENSIA: Ow, I really hurt myself. God, I'm getting dizzy. Oh, I'm breaking out in a cold sweat... Tell that harpy to get out of the bathroom because I've got to go in there. What a way to end the party!
LORENZO: Consuelito... *(CONSUELITO comes out. HORTENSIA approaches her but goes to pass by her. CONSUELITO grabs her and pushes her inside.)*
CONSUELITO: This way, you drunken sot. *(She locks the door with a key.)* I've set you free as a bird, love of my life.
LORENZO: This is some night...
HORTENSIA: *(From within.)* Oh...!
CONSUELITO: If that whore has her trunk, I've got my own little chest. Nobody's seen it but it's time I showed it to you. *(She looks around.)* Everything I have is kept in here... Well, not everything, now. *(She shows him a photo.)* Look, here I am at six months. *(Responding to his silence.)* How cute!...
LORENZO: *(In truth, without much interest.)* This?
CONSUELITO: No, that's the pillow. I'm the little naked thing on top of it. *(Changing over.)* Look, I'll get on the other side, because with that ear you can't hear a thing and let's not start shouting... I don't like these quiet romantic scenes at all, but we'll have time to raise our voices in Orleans... This doll's name is Marga. She's missing an eye but it's inside. *(She shakes it.)* You hear? Ah, what are you going to hear?... Look, locks of my hair. I'll give you some.
LORENZO: *(With a certain repugnance.)* What's this for?

CONSUELITO: Keep it. It'll bring you luck...
HORTENSIA: *(From within.)* Oh!
CONSUELITO: The day they cut it on me I cried a lot. More than when I got married. The ends of my braids hurt a lot. And I didn't even have them any more. With these little colored papers I used to paint my face... I had cinnamon colored cheeks. And blue shadow on my eyes. I was really pretty...
LORENZO: I can just picture you.
CONSUELITO: In Orleans I won't need that stuff. *(She throws the papers up in the air and shows him a photo.)* Look...
LORENZO: Who's this Indian?
CONSUELITO: That Indian is my mother, dressed up like a witch doctor... These shells are from a time we went to the beach.
HORTENSIA: *(From within.)* Open up!
CONSUELITO: Quiet! The three of us were so happy. My mother, my father, and me... When it came time to eat, all of a sudden we got caught in the biggest shower I ever saw in my life. What a mess! Our tortilla fell apart so you can just imagine. As far as the weather was concerned, my mother was an awful fortune teller. I remember my father kept slapping her on the back of the neck until we got under cover. The next day he woke up with pneumonia. It served him right: that's what you get for hitting a woman.
LORENZO: Don't you think he got it because he got soaked?
CONSUELITO: It could be, now that you mention it... Are you bored with me, Lorenzo?
LORENZO: Don't be ridiculous. It's fun being with you.
CONSUELITO: Thank you... My jump rope. *(She starts skipping rope.)*
LORENZO: Sssh. Don't make noise.
CONSUELITO: You're right. *(Like a little girl.)* Let's go to Orleans, Lorenzo. Let's go.
LORENZO: Yes. It's time to go... You shouldn't kill the goose that lays the golden eggs...
CONSUELITO: Did you say something about getting laid?
LORENZO: Forget it. We'll have to leave tomorrow.
CONSUELITO: *(Almost saddened.)* Tomorrow? So soon...? If you want, we can wait... If you're doing it just so I can skip rope... I shouldn't be doing any heavy exercise now... *(She sits down again.)* Ah, I'm going to tell you my little surprise from before. You know where I'm keeping it? *(Pointing to her stomach.)* Here.
LORENZO: *(Horrified.)* What?

CONSUELITO: Here, Lorenzo: I'm going to be a mother.
LORENZO: You... and me?
CONSUELITO: No, you're going to be a father. I'm going to be the mother. That's why I've been throwing up all over the place these days. *(A pause.)* Aren't you happy? Aren't you going to say anything?
LORENZO: I'm absolutely speechless.
CONSUELITO: I thought you would take it differently. Of course, there are a lot of people who are left speechless from joy. It's great, isn't it? What a good father you are! *(She takes his hand and places it on her stomach.)* Here's your father. Get to know him so you'll be able to get along. Here's your son, Lorenzo. His eyes are bigger than yours but he looks just like you... He'll be born in Orleans. You'll ring in the morning and I'll be giving birth near the bells. The baby will be frightened by all the noise but I'll say to him *(She is now holding the doll in her arms.)* : "Hush, hush; it's your father, doing what makes him happy." We'll take walks, arm in arm, pushing the baby carriage. The baby's name is Cleofás, if you don't mind. My husband was a good man... Anyway, just in case it bothers you, I'll call him Sultan. And he'll ride around in the carriage pointing at the clouds, because he wants to be an artist like his father. And you'll teach him... Like me... In Orleans everything is different...
LORENZO: *(With a touch of tenderness.)* You poor little thing!
CONSUELITO: Poor, no. I'll have my little chest with me. I'll carry my child around... I'm not poor. *(LORENZO passes his hand across her shoulder, through sympathy or attraction. To the doll:)* "Hush, hush: it's not war, you silly child. Hush up." *(Very tenderly, she begins to sing a lullaby:)*

> Your mama, she rides the trapeze.
> Your papa, he makes the bells ring.
> Your uncle, he is the sexton
> In the mass he's going to sing.
>
> God keep my child,
> Who's fast asleep
> As the bells ring in the morning.

(LORENZO, taken over by that something special of CONSUELITO, embraces her.) Not now, Lorenzo. Not now. Don't you see that he's just fallen asleep? *(And sweetly, ridiculously, marvelously, cradling the doll, with Lorenzo looking on in amazement, she enters CLEOFAS'S room.)*

DARKNESS

SCENE II

CONSUELITO, alone, comes out of her bedroom. She begins to busy herself dusting. When she gets to her chair, she caresses it a bit and begins to kiss it; she waves good-by to it.

CONSUELITO: Tarsi, you beautiful creature, today I'm leaving for Orleans. Why aren't you singing? *(CLEOFAS enters from the church. He looks at her silently for a moment. He has some candelabras with him.)*
CLEOFAS: Good morning.
CONSUELITO: You went out very early this morning. I didn't hear you get up. Where did you go?
CLEOFAS: To the river. I took a walk along the bank. The reeds were wet. Look at the way I've come back... And it was a clear day, nice and quiet. I've been thinking about a lot of things... *(He sits down and starts to clean the candelabras.)*
CONSUELITO: *(Who had gone for some slippers and hands them to him.)* Here. And bring me those shoes so I can dry them, otherwise the dampness will leave a stain. *(He does so.)* Why didn't you call me? You know how much I like to go down to the river.
CLEOFAS: That's where I saw you the first time. You don't remember. *(CONSUELITO remains still for a few seconds, with her back turned to him, attentive without wanting to be.)* I was looking for some sweet smelling herbs for the monument to Holy Thursday. You were sitting down, talking to yourself, with your feet dangling in the water.
CONSUELITO: I wasn't talking to myself. I was talking to Marga.
CLEOFAS: It was because of Marga that I didn't want to wake you up this morning. You were hugging her just like a little girl.
CONSUELITO: Her name is not Marga any more. And it's not a girl doll; it's a boy doll. His name is... *(She stops before saying the name.)* Well, I call him Sultan. When I was a teenager, I got a cat whose name was Sultan. He didn't love anybody but me. He disappeared one January. Then he came back a long time later, bleeding all over. He came back to die.
CLEOFAS: *(Beginning a series of parallel responses.)* The cloths on Santa Engracia's altar are full of dust.
CONSUELITO: *(With her hands over her stomach.)* His name was Sultan, too... I was a teenager...
CLEOFAS: We'll have to wash them one of these days.
CONSUELITO: One night we went to the San Pedro festival and you bought me a half dozen carnations. I still have them.

CLEOFAS: The choir loft is full of cobwebs. What do you say tomorrow we get a table and a broom and wipe them all up?
CONSUELITO: "If some day I find out you're cheating on me," you told me, "I'll shoot you first and then I'll shoot myself." I believed it, and then no shot or anything.
CLEOFAS: This time we'll make sure we've got the table anchored well so we won't have what happened in November... when you fell down on top of the organ. It made such a loud noise that three yards of the molding shook loose from the wall...
CONSUELITO: We'll have to put away this jacket. It's not going to be cold any more.
CLEOFAS: We'll do it tomorrow or the day after. What's the hurry? *(They look at each other an instant.)*
CONSUELITO: Tomorrow... *(Putting a cloth on her knees.)* Once you get stains on you with that metal cleaner, there's no way to get them off... By the way, it's better to brush off your cassock with a brush that's been dampened with warm tea. You understand? I've always done it that way. *(She goes to clean the cage.)* This is mine, isn't it?
CLEOFAS: *(He lifts up his eyes.)* It was the only thing you brought with you when we got married... *(He remains there remembering.)*
CONSUELITO: I think I'm going to let him go. He can't be happy in the cage. Let him take off, too.
CLEOFAS: *(In a low voice.)* What do you mean by "too?"
CONSUELITO: Let him find his own life, like Sultan, like everybody. Good-by, Tarsi. Go away, Tarsi. Birdseed isn't good for anything. There are lots of things better than birdseed... You selfish, gluttonous pig. If there was nobody around to feed you, you'd see how fast you'd go look for something.
CLEOFAS: Maybe he'll stay because... he loves his cage. There are lots of people like that. *(CONSUELITO feels a little dizzy.)* Consuelito, what's the matter? If you keep going from one place to another without stopping...
CONSUELITO: I just wanted to do a good job cleaning the house before... opening up the raffle.
CLEOFAS: The raffle is all over. We don't need it. Tomorrow I'm taking the stand down.
CONSUELITO: I'll help you. *(CONSUELITO cleans candelabras, taking the cleanser from the same container as CLEOFAS.)*
CLEOFAS: Where's my mother?
CONSUELITO: She went to the market.

CLEOFAS: And... Lorenzo?
CONSUELITO: I don't know. He left.
CLEOFAS: Was he carrying a bell?
CONSUELITO: I didn't notice.
CLEOFAS: You didn't notice if he was carrying a bell?
CONSUELITO: I saw it down here, taken from its spot.
CLEOFAS: *(Lying.)* The bell frame was loose. I sent him to have it fixed.
CONSUELITO: *(They look at each other.)* You sent him to do it?
CLEOFAS: No, the bell frame wasn't loose. And I didn't send him to do anything... In the end, the only important thing is that we have to die. It's a question of waiting for death with a little bit of company. There's no use kidding ourselves...
CONSUELITO: He thought we were playing a trick on him.
CLEOFAS: Who?
CONSUELITO: Tarsi. He thought we were going to shut the door to his cage as soon as he went to leave.
CLEOFAS: That happens to all of us... We almost get away sometimes. But somebody on the other side always winds up slamming the door in our face... The best we can do is fly from one cage to another one that's a little bit bigger.
CONSUELITO: Three-hundred and fifteen stars have been finished. But seventy-two of them still have to have their tails put on.
CLEOFAS: Don't worry about that.
CONSUELITO: But it's such a shame to see a star without a tail...
(HORTENSIA comes in from the street, in a complete furor.)
HORTENSIA: My head is killing me. Don't anybody say anything or I'll kill them. Right here, in the back of the head, I've got like a purple skull cap. Just like a bishop's. Ow! Don't anybody say even half a word. Where did all these candelabras come from?
CLEOFAS: From the crypt. I had them locked up.
HORTENSIA: I don't know why there's all this mistrust... Why would anybody want a candelabra? Let's see. *(She takes one.)*
CLEOFAS: Just in case...
HORTENSIA: I don't have any idea of what case you're talking about, but I don't like that tone of voice. And just to show you, take this. Enjoy it. It's from that Argentine nun. She says that my cousin, Sebi Laguna, went to his rest in the bosom of the Lord five days ago.
CLEOFAS: *Requiem aeternamm dona eis, Domine.*

HORTENSIA: *(In spite of herself.)* Et lux perpetua luceat ei. That bastard must be causing a hell of an uproar in the bosom of the Lord. Here, read this. *(She gives him the letter.)*
CLEOFAS: *(Reading.)* "The mission of our order is to care for hopeless patients without means. But since your cousin informed us that you are in a magnificent economic situation and he praised your charity..."
HORTENSIA: That nun must have swallowed everything hook, line and sinker.
CLEOFAS: "... we are taking the liberty of asking you for a donation for our hospital, for the memory and salvation of the soul of your cousin, Sebastián Laguna, who loved you very much."
HORTENSIA: Holy shit! Some American uncle he was!
CONSUELITO: *(To CLEOFAS.)* When you take down the purple altar cloths on Resurrection Day, don't put them away until you dust them off first.
HORTENSIA: I told you a hundred times I don't want anybody to talk to me. *(LORENZO appears in the doorway to the street. When he sees the other three he tries to draw back but CLEOFAS has seen him.)*
CLEOFAS: Good morning, Lorenzo.
LORENZO: *(Entering.)* Good morning. Did you have a good rest?
HORTENSIA: Rest! Resting in this house is getting to be very difficult.
LORENZO: What? *(Still, reticent, with his hand to his ear.)*
HORTENSIA: *(Shouting.)* I didn't get any rest! *(In pain, because of her shouting.)* Ow, my head.
LORENZO: I... I thought that at this time of day... there wouldn't be anybody here...
CLEOFAS: Yeah, I guess so...
LORENZO: And we've got a full house. *(Making the best of it.)*
CLEOFAS: We were waiting for you.
LORENZO: *(Taken aback.)* For me? Why?
CLEOFAS: Because we wanted you to hear a letter from the Bishop's Office. It's signed by the secretary.
HORTENSIA: Today is a big day for letters.
CLEOFAS: Here's what it says. *(He unfolds a sheet of paper.)* "In the name of his Excellency, the Bishop, I am pleased to inform you that in accordance with your request"--this letter is addressed to Don Remigio-- "you are relieved of your parish office for reasons of age and health, to be replaced by Don Manuel Castresana Ruiz, who will take possession of the parish next Saturday, the seventh day of the month."

HORTENSIA: That's all we needed. This is every man for himself. What did I tell you, Lorenzo? Do you see...?
LORENZO: And what... do you intend to do?
CLEOFAS: I haven't finished. *(Reading.)* "Likewise, His Excellency, the Bishop, has decided that Lorenzo Gutiérrez, the bellman of that parish, should be promoted, by virtue of his merits, to chief bellman of the ancient cathedral of Orleans..." You understand?
LORENZO: *(He lowers his eyes.)* Yes.
HORTENSIA: Orleans? But what kind of a mix-up is this? I must be the deaf one now. It must be my head.
CONSUELITO: Orleans... *(To CLEOFAS.)* Why didn't you tell me about this before?
CLEOFAS: It hadn't been decided yet. Up until today there was still some doubt in the Bishop's Office about whether to send Lorenzo or me to Orleans.
HORTENSIA: You? And we thought Don Remigio had a few screws loose. Compared with the Bishop, he's a genius. Anyway, I'll have to get used to the idea of Orleans. Long live tourism...
CLEOFAS: When are you leaving?
LORENZO: Well... I guess right now... if you think it's all right.
CLEOFAS: Of course, as soon as possible. These things should always be done as soon as possible.
LORENZO: I already have my suitcase packed.
CLEOFAS: I saw it this morning. But you forgot to put in your shaving things.
HORTENSIA: Wait a little while, Lorenzo, my boy. Everything's caught me so unexpected. Wait a while. *(She goes toward her room. CONSUELITO looks in her little chest. She puts away her doll. She repeatedly puts herself in the way of the movements made by LORENZO, who goes to the barber's shelf, takes his shaving gear and puts it in his suitcase, always with his eyes downcast. A pause.)*
CLEOFAS: Congratulations on the appointment. *(HORTENSIA comes out with a hastily wrapped package, which she puts away in her trunk.)*
HORTENSIA: Here's my luggage, Lorenzo. *(He ignores her. A pause.)* I said this is my trunk.
CLEOFAS: We've already heard you, Mama. *(LORENZO goes to leave. CONSUELITO gets in front of him at the door. CLEOFAS moves her away gently. A pause.)*
CONSUELITO: *(Not speaking to anyone in particular.)* I'm going to have a baby.

CLEOFAS: Lorenzo already knows, Consuelito... And he's very happy for you. Aren't you, Lorenzo? *(LORENZO makes a vague and embarrassed gesture.)*
HORTENSIA: I knew it. I didn't want to believe it, but I knew it. They've been laughing behind my back. Stop him, Cleofás. He's running away with our money. He's taking everything with him. That's what he was using the uniform for.
CLEOFAS: Calm down, Mama. You've got a headache.
HORTENSIA: I'm the one that gave him the money. I gave it to him...
CLEOFAS: Why would you give money to Lorenzo? Good-by, and thanks a lot for being such good company for the three of us. You did us a great favor by coming. Good-by. *(A pause. LORENZO leaves.)*
HORTENSIA: He's running away with everything! He's running away with everything! *(CONSUELITO, in a faint voice, sits down in her chair, with her back to everything. A pause.)*
CONSUELITO: Lorenzo... I was going to go to Orleans. *(CONSUELITO gets up.)*
HORTENSIA: Love arrives too late and it goes away too soon. The same thing always happens.
CLEOFAS: *(Going back to his candelabras.)* Love is nothing more than growing old together. All the rest is crap.
HORTENSIA: Yeah, yeah, crap... *(Skeptical in her answer.)* What's going to become of me? What'll I do tomorrow? And the day after tomorrow? And thirty years from now?
CLEOFAS: Thirty years from now you'll be nice and quiet. Like Doña Leonor. Until that time you'll do what everybody else does: begin each day all over.
CONSUELITO: In Orleans the houses are happy. The people smile and they stroll along the streets, window shopping...
CLEOFAS: Orleans is a lie!
CONSUELITO: *(Repeating something that someone has told her.)* The trees are tall and they have blue flowers. He told me that love, in Orleans... *(She can't go on.)*
CLEOFAS: In Orleans, it doesn't exist. Love is committing yourself and then going forward.
HORTENSIA: Well, listen to them, talking about love. How does that grab you? *(CONSUELITO gets up.)*
CLEOFAS: What are you going to do?
CONSUELITO: Make the tails for the seventy-two stars...
CLEOFAS: You'll have time for that. I have to ask you to forgive me.

HORTENSIA: Hey, I'm the one who should be asked for forgiveness... by everybody.
CLEOFAS: This morning I was ready to run away. To go down to the river and never come back again...
CONSUELITO: *(Who has sat down again.)* In Orleans all of us are good-looking and smart.
CLEOFAS: Orleans is a lie!
CONSUELITO: And happiness is like coffee and cream that you drink and forget everything. When we get to Orleans, they'll put a small child in our arms....
CLEOFAS: You can't be happy by dreaming. The only thing you do is lose days from your life: a good life or a bad life. Happiness is a job: I found that out this morning. You've got to open your eyes wide, not close them. And be wide awake. And yet, and yet...
HORTENSIA: *(Because they are not paying attention to her.)* I don't know what this would-be sermonizer is talking to me about.
CLEOFAS: I'm not talking to you, Mama. You're beyond hope.
HORTENSIA: *(In a more human tone.)* I lived through times when happiness left me out in the cold. I always lived for life. And look at me...
CONSUELITO: We didn't like our life, the same day after day. In Orleans we were going to be different.
CLEOFAS: This is what we are. They used to tell us: "And the princess married the prince." There aren't any princesses. There aren't any princes. Everything has its price and you have to learn how to pay it.
CONSUELITO: *(Who has broken a star tail.)* We didn't like these butterfingers. They broke everything. They played a dirty trick on me...
CLEOFAS: Life doesn't play tricks on us. Dreams play tricks on us, Consuelito. *Procul recedant somnium.*
HORTENSIA: No matter how much Latin you know, the trouble with you is you'll always be a left-winger.
CLEOFAS: The trouble with me is the trouble with everybody: I don't want to be left all alone.
HORTENSIA: Cut the crap. The only thing I know is I've got one foot in the grave and everybody's been laughing behind my back. Goddamn letter; if it wasn't for that, at least I wouldn't have known. *(She goes to rip up the letter CLEOFAS left on the table.)* Hey! This is your handwriting! You wrote it! This letter is not from the Bishop's Office. I was starting to wonder about all that fuss over Orleans... What have you done? You stupid idiot!

CLEOFAS: It's all the same, Mama. He was going to leave. The only thing I did was to open the door for him so he wouldn't have to go through the window. Con artists are always like that: they fish in troubled waters. If the current changes, they take their gear someplace else. Their job is to take advantage of other people's fears, of their weaknesses.
HORTENSIA: *(Grabbing the handle of her trunk.)* Well, I'm not afraid. And I'm not weak. I'm leaving. *(She waits for her son to stop her.)* I said I'm leaving.
CLEOFAS: Leave. You'll know exactly where to find him. In some antique shop, selling what he took away, little by little. You're the only antique he didn't want... *(Trying to hurt her.)*
HORTENSIA: Is that the way you talk to your mother?
CLEOFAS: *(Finishing the matter.)* You're not a mother just because you bring people into the world... *(To CONSUELITO.)* And you're not a father just because you made a baby, but because of all the other things that come later...
CONSUELITO: In Orleans the stars are made out of star...
HORTENSIA: *(Trying to salvage a deal.)* All right. For the time being nothing has changed in the parish, either. After all this indignation, that's not a bad bit of news...
CLEOFAS: The parish will change sooner or later. It doesn't matter any more.
HORTENSIA: *(As if coming across a great discovery.)* Wait! Now I get it, my son. How clever. We can say that the bellman disappeared with everything that's missing. And we wash our hands of it. Let them set the bloodhounds on the bastard. I hope they find him in Orleans. *(She laughs.)* We were the first to suffer damages. Who would have suspected?... Whoever said you were dumb, Cleofás?
CLEOFAS: It won't be like that either. I finally feel free. I don't care who comes. What we've done isn't too serious: we tried to live. So what? They can kick us out of here... *(A gesture of indifference.)* The world doesn't end in the chapel of Santo Tomé. Maybe it ends from that door in, where we've been wasting so many of our good days between these walls, which also had their own good days. Trying to patch things up and put in kitchen sinks and toilets: living in a place that wasn't made for all that... In the middle of so much solemnity, everything turns out phony: even the bread, even this jar...
CONSUELITO: Orleans!

CLEOFAS: And what's phony are all the other things. This morning, as I was going along the river I was thinking how we dream about the best of all worlds: a palace of plastic...
CONSUELITO: Orleans!
CLEOFAS: Crazy. We're crazy! When they kick me out, I'll fight my way through the streets until the baby is born. Let him be born right in the middle of the street, free to choose his own parish, or not to choose any. And if happiness comes, fine. If it doesn't, the hell with it. And, in the end, we'll straighten it out with whoever is there...
CONSUELITO: The baby was going to be named Cleofás...
HORTENSIA: *(To CONSUELITO, in a cutting way.)* The baby's going to be a girl!
CLEOFAS: If it's a girl her name will be Esperanza, because she'll have hope... *(To CONSUELITO, with her Marga.)* Where are you going?
CONSUELITO: I'm going to ring the Angelus bell...
HORTENSIA: *(Shouting.)* It's not the right time!
CLEOFAS: *(To defend CONSUELITO.)* It's always the right time for that.
HORTENSIA: Besides, there aren't any bells! The last one was just sold! *(Responding defiantly to CLEOFAS.)* You heard me!
CLEOFAS: *(To CONSUELITO.)* There aren't any more bells, Consuelito...
CONSUELITO: *(Shrugging her shoulders.)* I'll ring them in Orleans.
CLEOFAS: Don't talk nonsense. Come here...
CONSUELITO: *(Refusing.)* I have to go up...
CLEOFAS: But where are you going?
CONSUELITO: To Orleans.
HORTENSIA: *(Cruelly.)* A lot of attention she pays to you!
CLEOFAS: *(To his mother, being distracted a few seconds from CONSUELITO, who is self-absorbed and who keeps on climbing.)* Shut up!
HORTENSIA: Who are you to order me around?
CLEOFAS: The head of the family.
HORTENSIA: And what am I? The asshole?
CLEOFAS: Shut up!
CONSUELITO: *(In a soft voice.)* In Orleans nobody fights...
CLEOFAS: It's not time for the Angelus... Come down, Consuelito!
CONSUELITO: In Orleans it's always noontime.
CLEOFAS: Come down! Orleans is a lie!
CONSUELITO: No... It's true... It's the only thing that's true...
(CONSUELITO goes up out of sight. CLEOFAS runs after her. Her last words are heard from offstage.)

CLEOFAS: Come back, Consuelito. Wait... No! Not that! *(He comes down immediately, dejected and devastated. He looks at HORTENSIA. A pause.)* She... She fell.
HORTENSIA: *(Looking at him.)* Sure, sure... she fell. Now they'll open up an investigation! *(After a few seconds, CLEOFAS, without hesitating any longer, runs out into the street.)* Oh, what an idiot she was, right to the end! She wasn't good for anything, not even for living! *(The grand bell strokes of the Angelus start to ring.)* What are those bells? A miracle! Thank you, Lord. *(In a perverse tone.)* At least there's something left to sell! *(In mock tragedy, going toward the street.)* Consuelito, my child! What a horrible accident!

(She leaves. After a few seconds, during which the stage seems empty and meaningless, the voice of DON REMIGIO is heard: "Fellow parishioners... fellow parishioners..." In the meantime, there is a slow falling of the curtain)

CURTAIN

THE END

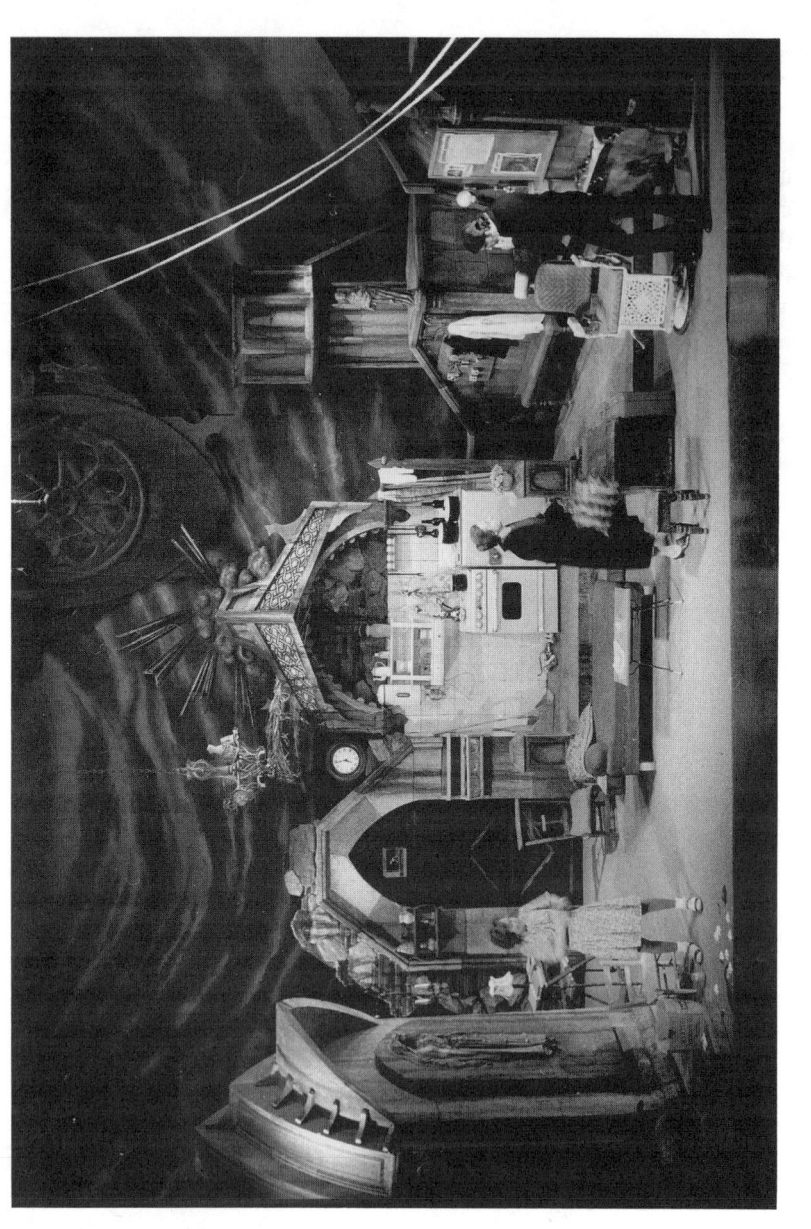

Original 1972 production of *Los buenos días perdidos*. Photo by Manuel Martínez Muñoz.

CRITICAL REACTION

On the 1972 Madrid opening:

The first act of this very personal lyric poem could have lasted another hour without wearing down the audience. The unpretentious and unpredictable dialog, full of "Galistic" wit and poetic touches, is the great spectacle of this wonderful piece... The entire [...work...] is a stylized Iberian delight, playful in the best literary and ethnic traditions, rich in amusing double entendres, expressive verbal dexterity, abundant vocabulary and surprises... How beautiful theater sounds when beyond the spectacle, stupendous as this one is, there is a great text and a great writer!

Nuevo Diario, October 12, 1972

The Bells of Orleans comes wrapped in a brilliantly comic package. The author machine-guns the audience with a dazzling display of... clever, sassy and irreverent repartees [that] have the spectators rolling in laughter. But they can't get out of their minds the wretched essence of the characters... Against this background... Antonio Gala plants his sparkling dialog, which makes us laugh but which in no way hides the sordid and carnival-like framework of the story's tragedy.

ABC, October 12, 1972

On the 1991 Madrid revival:

The work has more than enough literary merits to transcend what could have wound up being a testimony to a situation anchored in a period of time... In putting on The Bells of Orleans it is difficult to add anything new to the script because it has it all, overflowing with a fine range of sentiments: the misery of some hopeless lives and the capacity of human beings to dream; the tragedy to which the characters of this "Spanish story" are drawn and the feeling of "living above it all" that pulls at them, arousing in the audience a fluctuation of emotions which run from compassion to the most unrestrained laughter.

Rosalía Gómez
El Público/84, May-June, 1991

ABOUT THE TRANSLATOR

Edward E. Borsoi is Professor of Foreign Languages at Rollins College and teaches courses in Spanish, Italian and Linguistics. He is the co-author of *Tertulia,* an intermediate Spanish textbook, and has published *Poemas a España,* a translation of William Wordsworth's *Poems Dedicated to National Independence and Liberty* . He has recently completed an English translation of *Festino nella sera del Giovedì Grasso avanti cena,* the libretto of a musical work by the seventeenth century Italian composer Adriano Banchieri.

TRANSLATOR'S ACKNOWLEDGEMENTS

I would like to express my thanks to Martha T. Halsey for her assiduousness in undertaking the Estreno translation series and for providing me with the honor of participating in a series with such prestigious scholars. In addition, I would like to state my appreciation to Antonio Gala for his creative talents, his hospitality, and his patience. Above all, I owe an enormous debt of gratitude to Phyllis Zatlin for her constant generosity in sharing her expertise and insights with me, for the incredible amount of time and energy she contributed to this project, and for her enthusiasm and encouragement in guiding me.

E.E.B.

ESTRENO: CUADERNOS DEL TEATRO ESPAÑOL CONTEMPORANEO

Published at Penn State University
Martha Halsey, Ed.
Phyllis Zatlin, Assoc. Ed.

    A journal featuring play texts of previously unpublished works from contemporary Spain, interviews with playwrights, directors, and critics, and extensive critical studies in both Spanish and English.

    Plays published have included texts by Buero-Vallejo, Sastre, Arrabal, Gala, Nieva, Salom, Martín Recuerda, Olmo, Martínez Mediero, F. Cabal, P. Pedrero and Onetti. The journal carries numerous photographs of recent play performances in Spain and elsewhere, including performances in translation.

    Also featured are an annual bibliography, regular book reviews, and critiques of the recent theater season, as well as a round table in which readers from both the U. S. and Spain share information and engage in lively debates.

    ESTRENO also publishes a series of translations of contemporary Spanish plays which may be subscribed to separately.

Please mail to: ESTRENO
350 N. Burrowes Bldg.
University Park, PA 16802
USA.

Individual subscriptions are $14.00 and institutional subscriptions, $26.00 for the calendar year.

Name   _____

Address   _____
                          _____

ESTRENO: CONTEMPORARY SPANISH PLAYS SERIES

General Editor: Martha T. Halsey

No. 1   Jaime Salom: *Bonfire at Dawn* (*Una hoguera al amanecer*)
         Translated by Phyllis Zatlin. 1992.

No. 2   José López Rubio: *In August We Play the Pyrenees* (*Celos del aire*)
         Translated by Marion P. Holt. 1992.

No. 3   Ramón del Valle-Inclán: *Savage Acts: Four Plays* (*Ligazón, La rosa de papel, La cabeza del Bautista, Sacrilegio*)
         Translated by Robert Lima. 1993.

No. 4   Antonio Gala: *The Bells of Orleans* (*Los buenos días perdidos*)
         Translated by Robert Borsoi. 1993.

No. 5   Antonio Buero-Vallejo: *The Music Window* (*Música cercana*)
         Translated by Marion P. Holt. 1994.

No. 6   Paloma Pedrero: *Parting Gestures: Three by Pedrero* (*El color de agosto, La noche dividida, Resguardo personal*)
         Translated by Phyllis Zatlin. 1994.

A continuing series representing Spanish plays of several generations and varying theatrical approaches, selected for their potential interest to American audiences. Published every 6-9 months. Forthcoming plays will include works of Ana Diosdado, Manuel Martínez Mediero, Alonso Vallejo, and others.

SUBSCRIPTION/ORDER FORM

Check one:

_____ Standing order for play series. (May be cancelled at any time if desired.) $6.00 including postage, to be billed when you receive your copy.

_____ Individual play/s. List titles and quantities below:

_____ _____

Please include payment at $6.00 per copy, postpaid.

_____ _____

Name and address: _____

_____

_____

Mail to: ESTRENO
350 N. Burrowes Bldg.
University Park, PA 16802 USA

Telephone: 814/865-1122
FAX: 814/863-7944

PLAYS OF THE NEW DEMOCRATIC SPAIN (1975-1990)

Contents

Editor's Prologue   Patricia W. O'Connor
Introduction   Felicia Londré

Eloise Is Under an Almond Tree (Eloísa está debajo de un almendro), by Enrique Jardiel Poncela; Steven Capsuto, translator

Bitter Lemon (La piel del limón), by Jaime Salom; Patricia O'Connor, translator

The Audition (El verí del teatre), by Rudolf Sirera; John London, translator

Bikes Are for Summer (Las bicicletas son para el verano), by Fernando Fernán-Gómez; Dale Hartkemeyer, translator

Going Down to Marrakesh (Bajarse al moro), by José Luis Alonso de Santos; Phyllis Zatlin, translator

Lazarus in the Labyrinth (Lázaro en el laberinto), by Antonio Buero-Vallejo; Hazel Cazorla, translator

Hardback .... 57.58 (+ tax)
Paperback .... 32.50 (+ tax)*
* Special discount for Estreno readers:
Paperback 28.00

Orders:

Estreno
Department of Romance Languages (ML 377)
University of Cincinnati
Cincinnati, OH 45221
U. S. A.